How to Get a Job

in Sports

by
Dale Ratermann and Mike Mullen

MASTERS PRESS

A Division of Howard W. Sams & Company
A Bell Atlantic Company

Masters Press (A Division of Howard W. Sams & Co.)
2647 Waterfront Parkway, East Drive, Suite 300
Indianapolis, IN 46214

© Dale Ratermann and Mike Mullen

Library of Congress Cataloging-in-Publication Data

Ratermann, Dale, 1956-
   How to get a job in sports / Dale Ratermann and Mike Mullen
      p. cm.
      ISBN: 1-57028-043-6: $12.95
      1. Sports--Vocational guidance--United States.
      I. Mullen, Mike, 1951.
      II. Title

GV583.R38   1995
796.023--dc20   95-44701
                                                        CIP

Credits:
Edited by Kim Heusel
Text layout by Kim Heusel
Cover design by Phil Velikan
Cover Photo by Suzanne Lincoln

Illustrations © CorelDRAW!

Acknowledgments

Thanks to the following for their contributions to this book: Kim Heusel, Holly Kondras and Tom Bast at Masters Press, and the many professionals in the sports industry who have graciously offered their expertise.

About the Authors

Dale Ratermann is vice president of administration for the Indiana Pacers. He has worked in sports for more than 20 years after getting his first internship at the University of Illinois athletic department.

Mike Mullen is president and CEO of ProBasketball Electronic Services Inc., and maintains the largest sports segment on the information superhighway. He received his first job in sports through a temporary employment service.

Table of Contents

1 — Crazy About Sports 1

2 — What Exactly Do You Want? 15

3 — A Gold Mine of Insider Advice 31

4 — Resumé Do's and Don'ts 53

5 — Personal Interview Do's and Don'ts 73

6 — Where Do You Go From Here? 79

7 — Sometimes, It's "WHO YOU KNOW" 89

1

Crazy About
Sports

Are you one of those people who just loves sports? Do you turn to the sports pages before reading the news headlines? If you own a computer, do you check out the sports chat sessions and box scores as soon as you log on to the information highway? When you go to the shopping mall with your family, do you find yourself browsing the television department in order to watch the big game while your family strolls away? Have you ever named a pet dog after a sports team or idol? Do you invite friends over for sports parties when your favorite team is on TV fighting for a playoff spot? Perhaps you go to a sports bar to watch an event with friends, or even strangers, just to be a part of a sports crowd.

If your answer to all, any or some of the above is yes, keep reading. This book may change your life. Of course, what you actually do with your life is up to you, but if you listen to what you are saying, consider a career in sports.

The luckiest people in the working world are those who get paid for having fun. Think about what you enjoy in life then find out how to make a career out of it.

Ask yourself: Is sports my hobby?

Remember how you used to play on the local team? Or keep stats? Maybe you were the equipment manager because you didn't have the talent to be on the field but just wanted to do something to be a part of the team.

Maybe you are a female who never had the opportunity to play professionally but would like to get involved somehow in the front office. Are you one of the millions of kids who collected trading cards for every sport, or at least all the cards in your favorite sport? Do you find yourself making friends with other sports fans? Do your conversations revolve around sports?

Keep reading. You sound like you've got a serious case of sportsitis.

Let's face it: We have to work most of our lives doing something. Wouldn't it be great to actually enjoy waking up early in the morning and heading off to work? Or staying late without complaining, even volunteering to leave after your normal quitting time without seeking overtime pay?

It's true. In the sports industry, you could discover that you actually prefer being at work because it's a "happening" atmosphere. Sports happens.

Maybe sports should be happening for you, too. If you've read this far, you are a strong candidate for a career in sports. In fact, you can probably think of many scenarios in which sports dominates your life in some way.

The reality is, you're crazy about sports. You dream about a career in sports, but just don't know how to get your foot in the door of a professional sports team.

That, fellow sports fanatic, is the purpose of this book. You can have that career if you have a sincere desire and a good work ethic. All you need is a career plan and someone to point you in the right direction.

Don't misunderstand. No book can guarantee a job. You can't expect that from anything or anybody. You are the only one who can guarantee your success. But the opportunities abound if you know where to look and know how to approach the right people at the right moment. Hopefully, this book will enlighten you to some vital do's and don'ts. You'll meet some stiff competition along the way, but don't fret. Sports organizations need good, experienced people.

Experienced? Yes, experienced. But don't let that scare you. After all, isn't that why you're reading this book? Experience has to start somewhere, and the sporting industry is booming like never before, with new leagues, teams and sports popping up like wild flowers. Your chance to get that elusive experience has never been greater.

The sporting industry has skyrocketed into the Top 20 list of the most lucrative business fields in the world. If you think YOU are crazy about sports, you're not alone. Take a look around. The whole planet, it seems, is bonkers over the business of sports and recreation, and a slew of related enterprises.

The most watched television broadcasts of all time are those of major sporting events. Any broadcast network fortunate enough to have outbid the competition for the rights to a big game is assured of victory in its ratings war for the week. Other stations surrender and play old reruns of cheap B-movies rather than go up against the big game. The world is tuned in when it comes to sports. Or maybe vice versa. The rest of the world is tuned out when people tune in sports.

Sports makes people forget their hard day at the office and the problems of the world, or it helps them cast away the situations beyond control that seem to eat away at today's populace. In a world filled with stress, sports just seems to grow bigger and bigger as people from all nations, cultures, backgrounds and religions leave their problems at the gate and enter the sometimes surreal world it creates. Sports is the modern-day great escape.

To this extreme, it might appear at times as if "Old Man Logic" has been relegated to the "cheap seats" when it comes to sports. There is a magical air about sports that often brings its superstars more recognition than heads of state. Come to think of it, many retired sports stars have become political leaders. And dare we talk about the numbers of movie stars or broadcasters who ventured into their newfound careers because of high batting averages or great jump shots? To the non-sports fan, it would appear ludicrous to elect officials or to cast movies based upon past sports statistics, but to the fanatic, not only is it natural, it's a way to ingest more sports into daily life.

What is it about this thing called *sports*? Why would otherwise sane men shave their heads, but for either joining the military or for attending a major sporting event? Why do grown men and women paint their faces for something other than Halloween? What inspires a corporate vice president to rip a $1,000 suit diving for a $3 baseball? Why do people congregate in cold, rainy parking lots all night to cook sausages on the tailgates of station wagons?

It makes no sense.

Nonetheless, it's this craziness that offers you an opportunity for a career in sports. Possibly at this very moment, while you are reading this book, someone, somewhere, is starting a new business venture in the sporting industry, perhaps in areas you never knew existed. For example, the TV weather forecaster issues a blizzard warning advising people to stay indoors. Do they? If they are sports fans, no way. Voilá! A new capitalist venture springs forth, when an observant manufacturer introduces thermal hind side warmers for the 100,000 football fans who think sitting in blizzards is fun.

Why? What makes the sports fan thrive? Why does he return again and again? If you are a fanatic, you already know the answer.

Adrenaline.

Lots and lots of *sporting event* adrenaline, produced perhaps for one brief second in time, or more aptly by today's time clocks, for a few *tenths* of a second. In that brief adrenaline rush, the home-town fans exclaim, "This team gives me a heart attack." Then they open their wallets and buy another ticket for the next game. It is the speeding adrenaline that makes sports so unique. It is a cold rush that can produce no real damage if your team loses (except for tears running down the cheeks of 300-pound players 7 feet tall). In victory, it is a hot rush branching into every blood vessel so that you never forget the sensation of winning a magnificent battle. Sports adrenaline is a harmless addiction that allows no choice but to come back again and again for one more dose. It causes the sick to arise, as players and fans alike apply patchwork fixes to their bodily ills so they can attend the big game and get the juices flowing.

Sports adrenaline brings colorful celebration to the blind, and maddening roars to the deaf. And sometimes deafening roars to the mad. It brings rich and poor to the same table for a cheap dog and a brew. It quells racism, the only color barriers erected being the colors of the home team versus those of the visitors, good guys versus bad, be they black or white, male or female. It's US against THEM.

Sports adrenaline is the fire that allows football fanatics to remove their shirts in subzero weather and feel nothing but the sweat dripping down their brows. It's keeps seldom-seen relatives from boredom at Thanksgiving dinner while watching the Packers and Lions banging it out in the trenches.

Most of all, sports adrenaline is the *paint* used to create dreams passed down from one generation to the next in vivid color as Grandpa recalls the time he saw Babe Ruth hit his 60th home run (along with the 20 million other people who were at Yankee Stadium that day). Even the mere fantasy of having had a ticket to see Babe Ruth supplies a lifetime of harried heartbeats that only beat louder with time. So it doesn't matter that you pay a scalper $200 for a $9 seat . . . it's a bargain. Logic be gone! This is *sports*!

◆　　　　◆　　　　◆

As case in point, let's look back at the exciting Game 4 of the 1995 NBA Eastern Conference Finals between the Orlando Magic and Indiana Pacers at Market Square Arena in Indianapolis. Imagine the flood of adrenaline in a game which produced four lead changes and apparent game-winning shots within the final 15 seconds . . . a virtual roller coaster of agony and ecstasy.

The youthful Magic, led by superstars Shaquille O'Neal and Anfernee Hardaway held a 2-games-to-1 lead over the Pacers. A win by the Magic would surely put the Pacers on the doorstep of elimination. A win by the Pacers would bring the series back to a dead heat.

It's bedlam even before the game starts. Logic and reason stay home, while crazed fans become part of the spectacle. It's "prime time" *sports*.

There is much more to the game, than the GAME; much more to sports, than the SPORT. A television *sports crew* is outside the *sports arena*, sponsoring free head-shaves for Pacers fans, while Boomer, the *sports mascot,* leads a ragtime band and other *sports entertainment* across the street at the city market where the food court is open overtime for the event.

To the uninformed non-fans, *ticket brokers* (scalpers) are legally robbing sports enthusiasts who don't already have seats, but the avid fan appreciates the service and would gladly sell Mom to get one. People pay *sports makeup artists* to have their faces painted blue-and-gold. Newspaper vendors hawk *special sports editions*.

Local industry grinds to a halt, as companies shut down business early to let their employees join the pandemonium. The bank president is the one waving the sign, and the company janitor sells him a $12 seat for six hundred bucks. The mayor, dressed in a decorative show of support, enforces a blockade of the town's main thoroughfares so the bank president and the entire board of directors don't dance into oncoming traffic. The *arena management* employs extra *crowd control* to protect the thousands of others who rant and rave, and buy and sell their wares in the middle of the street during rush-hour traffic.

National broadcasting companies anchor their mobile trucks and point their receiving dishes toward the satellites in outer space. They've paid $800 million for the right to broadcast the games, but in return, they receive $900,000 for each 30 seconds of air time to sell beer and canvas shoes.

Mommies and daddies buy the kiddies a dinner of corn dogs and sodas from independent vendors who have set up shop outside to cater to the hungry mob who have shunned dinner at home in order to assemble outside *hours* before game time. Other vendors sell T-shirts with the latest funny phrase, while local radio stations give away promotional items.

Finally the doors open, and 17,000 sports lunatics stream into the building together, while those without tickets congregate in *sports* bars and *sports* clubs and *sports* restaurants where they party and watch the game on pay television on the *sports* channel.

Inside, the multi-billion dollar sports promotions industry takes control. They tell the referees to delay a little longer — they're introducing their new television summer lineup to the viewers, and the *sports drink* company has paid a small fortune to explain why it is the elixir of life.

The hamburger company has paid the sponsorship sales director to announce that if the Pacers win and hold their opponents to less than 100 points everyone can have a free hamburger. The pizza company wants the mascot to give away free pizzas; the airline, free vacation packages; the local car dealer, free rentals. The grocery store will give all the ladies a turkey if they hit a foul shot; selected fans can win fabulous prizes if they spin around in circles and try to throw the ball in the hoop.

Others can win T-shirts if they find a winning ticket under their seats with the gum. And if everyone will please watch the center scoreboard for the animated car race, all those in attendance having the winning car color will receive a free bag of chips from the local snack food company. If they'll watch the court, they can see the national beer company's *sports promotions* team of gymnasts bouncing off trampolines and into the basket. And save your ticket stub because the local clubs will give you free admission after the game, while restaurants and department stores will give you a 10 percent discount on steaks and *sportswear*.

Sports is a non-stop entertainment craze. It's a happening unlike any other.

The executive TV producer nods to the officials that the players can begin, and the game starts with the stipulation that if the coaches don't soon call a time-out the network will call one for them. Sports is big business and requires time to conduct business. Keep in mind, however, that if you work in sports, the time-out is NOT meant for YOU.

While television hawks its products, the fans inside are never put to rest. The carefully planned *game log* calls for the well-rehearsed dance team (cheerleaders are out — professional dancers are in) to spark the crowd during the first time-out, for the dog to catch Frisbees during the second time-out, for the beer gymnasts to jump over the backboard on the third time-out, for the dancers to entertain again at the end of the quarter, for the turkey shooters to come down from the stands at halftime, for the mascot to throw pizzas to the crowd during free throws, for the sound director to blast lively music during out-of-bounds plays, and for fans to look at the lucky numbers on their tickets, programs and seat locations for exciting prizes. The game isn't the only aspect of basketball that is clocked in the tenths of seconds — the entertainment also squeezes out every moment of time.

Now, it's the fourth quarter and the Pacers have a two-point lead, 89-87, with 15 seconds to go. Everyone's going to win a hamburger, a pizza, or a half-priced ticket to the comedy club. If only the home team can hold the lead for one more shot, the family can go celebrate. You can goof-around all day at work tomorrow. You can win that bet with cousin Billy in Orlando. The city mayor won't have to sit in the "dunk tank," while the mayor of Orlando throws balls at him. YOU CAN PARTY IN THE STREETS ALL NIGHT!

Only 15 seconds stand between you and ecstasy. It's something you've DREAMED about all your life, and it's in living color, right before your eyes.

Orlando throws the ball down low. No problem — you and 17,000 others have been screaming a warning of this scenario. You've told every player on the home team what to look for — Shaq in the middle. Cover Anderson and Scott for the three when Shaq dishes it back out.

Adrenaline!

This is why you've been a season-ticket buyer for years, struggling through the bad times for this 15-second rush that is unmatched in any other industry. This last 15 seconds are why entire companies closed down for a day and wasted countless hours all week at the water cooler, why students coughed up their meager part-time pay checks for a ticket, why adults took a cut in pay to skip work early...for this 15 seconds of sports adrenaline.

Oh, no! Shaq throws the ball to the substitute, Brian Shaw. He's not even supposed to be *in* the game, let alone shoot the GWS (game-winning shot). HE'S ALL ALONE! Nothing but net. Three-pointer. Orlando 90, Indiana 89. They win. We lose.

You quit breathing. Your heart stops. Your lungs drown on what once was adrenaline, now turned to vinegar. You're going to lay awake all night, unable to sleep, wondering what would have happened had you yelled loudly enough for your team to see Shaw wide open. Your life is ruined — if only you had worn the same lucky shirt that you wore to the last game; they've never lost when you've worn the lucky shirt. Your friend had insisted on repeating that silly voodoo spell that she hexed Orlando with for the last game, but no, you mocked her, and that's the reason for the loss.

Fans are as much to blame as the players, when a loss occurs. Fans must do everything exactly the same as they did when the team won the last game, or else defeat is inevitable. Superstitions are generally silly, except with sports, where they have been scientifically proven effective. Maybe somewhere in the hills of Southern Indiana, John Doe hadn't yelled, "MISS IT MISS IT MISS IT," loudly enough at his television. Now the Pacers — and you — have paid the ultimate cost . . . defeat. All your joy has been wiped away with a split-second defensive error.

The game isn't officially over, yet, but it might as well be over. Maybe a last-ditched prayer to God could turn it around. It will certainly take a miracle if you expect to pull this one out. Only 5.3 seconds to go and Reggie Miller is the only *go-to* guy on the court. He'll never even touch the ball. Maybe next year.

HEY REGGIE'S GOT IT! HE'S OPEN! HE GOT THE SHOT AWAY FOR A THREE!

OH MY GOD! IT WENT IN!

WE WIN!

WE WIN!

WE WIN!

BOOM BABY!

Sports adrenaline!

You haven't danced in years, yet now you are dancing in the aisle, hugging the people next to you and you don't even know them. Cheering so loudly you can't even hear.

WE WIN!

WE WIN!

WE WIN!

The boss will give you a big raise, the secretary a big kiss, the dog will give you an old bone he's dug up for an occasion such as this and...

OH, GOD, NO!

PENNY HARDAWAY IS WIDE OPEN . . . and he drains the three. We lose. We were so close to victory. It's a shame to have lost this way — it's better to get massacred than to have victory snatched from your taste buds. Seventeen thousand people hush, sitting down, stunned. Nobody talks. The shock of having your supply of sports adrenaline cut off in midstream is too tough to handle. There are no words for such a letdown. The team captain had told everyone that "Destiny" had predetermined them to win. Had he been wrong?

Say good-bye to that pay raise, and in truth, the boss will probably fire you. You'll probably kick the dog when you go home, and by the way, what did you do to God to have made him so mad at you.

It's your fault the team lost. You always eat spaghetti when the team needs a big win, and you didn't do it — just had to have that bratwurst outside, instead. That's what did it. And the green briefs — you can't be wearing anything at all green — it goes back to the Celtics game, when you caused the Pacers to win by removing your green sweater at halftime seven years ago. Well, maybe next year, but you just hate to lose . . .

HEY, THEY GOT THE BALL TO SMITS AT 15 FEET! HE SHAKES, BAKES, AND FAKES TREE ROLLINS OFF HIS FEET AT 0:00:1 ON THE CLOCK. HE GETS IT OFF! HE GETS IT OFF . . . IT'S IN!

IT'S GOOD! WAIT, DOES IT COUNT? WAS IT IN TIME?

YES! YES! YES!

WE WIN!

WE WIN!

WE WIN!

And that is why the world is bonkers over sports. That is why you want your career to be sports. For 15 seconds sports is EVERY-THING! Sports is how you sleep at night, how you behave at work, the town's attitude toward one another, and how you treat your dog. That is why athletes are idolized, and that is why the sporting industry generates billions of dollars a year.

Sports is king. Sports is an advertising battleground. Sports is a restaurant's special event. Sports is a clothing department. Sports is a gift shop's bread and butter. Sports is something you wear on your feet. Sports is something you drink. Sports is your baby's new rattle, and your toddler's action figure. In fact, you would be hard-pressed to find an industry that is not affected in one way or another by the local team's successes or failures.

Having a sports franchise in town is often a major determining factor when a corporation decides where to put its headquarters. Sports is often why a huge convention is held at a specific site, on a specific day, once again bringing in thousands of dollars. Sports events help cab drivers buy Christmas gifts for the kids, help tour guides to pay college tuition, help senior citizens who usher the games, and provide unemployed ticket-brokers with jobs.

Families choose vacation destinations based upon sports events and scheduling. Students and their parents often select educational institutions based upon, not scholastic achievements, but upon sports programs and winning traditions. Forget about the professor — who is the coach and what is his record?

And if Mom and Dad want to make sure you won't return their gift for something else, they place an official logo under the tree, regardless of what product the logo is on. The sports logo makes you actually *want* that tie, or coffee mug, or briefs, or socks, or key chain, or toilet seat. It's just your color or size, too. One size fits all.

It's sports. In fact, if environmentalists wanted to empty the nation's landfills, they would forget about recycling efforts, and simply put a sports logo on that old, worn car tire. Dad would keep it ... it's an official *sports* tire.

You simply can't go wrong with sports. Sports is the stuff of which dreams are made.

◆   ◆   ◆

You've made up your mind. You *love* sports. So much, in fact, that you seriously desire a *career* in sports. Imagine, getting *paid* to associate up close and personal with a game that millions annually shell out big bucks just to see from a distance.

At one point in life, *you* had lofty goals of being the star athlete. In fact, after your team's victory in the big game, you probably go home and dream that the raucous crowd chanted *your* name in celebration of the game-winning shot. But somewhere along the path of life, you got off the track to your athletic goals. Now you relive your glory days of high school by purchasing that ticket to the big game, and rewriting the script at night with *you* as the star. That is why the crowd does not want to readily leave the arena when the home team wins a heroic game — they each want to absorb the scene in preparation of the evening's dreams.

It's while lingering at your seat after the game that you notice the guy in the blue suit, sitting underneath the basket where the players congregate, rolling on the floor in jubilation. Hey, that's quite a job that guy's got, you think. What's he doing down there? How'd he get a dream job like that, anyway. Matter of fact, YOU wouldn't mind having a job like that, yourself!

Hey, that guy down there is jumping onto the piles of players, too. He's rolling on the floor with the superstars. What the heck does he do, anyway?

That does it. You go home, scratch up a resumé and fire it off to every team in the league, telling them how much you love basketball, and that you're willing to do *anything*, in any position, just to get a foot in the door before you move up the ladder to general manager in two seasons. You tell your family and friends that you're going to get a plush front office job doing . . . whatever it was that guy in the blue suit was doing.

By the start of next season, you're still waiting for a response to your resumé. What happened? Don't they understand how much you love basketball? It's all you've ever dreamed of since you were a kid. Maybe the post office lost your 29 resumés. Probably. Well, baseball is fun, too. Why not fire off 30-something more resumés, counting the local AAA team that you'd be willing to work a season or two for, while waiting for the Majors to call you up. Too bad, but the stupid post office lost all of your resumés again. Not one single response, except for the Yankees, who said thanks for asking, but they're just not hiring now. However, they're going to keep your resumé filed on the Director's desk for six months, and he will give you a call later, when something opens up in . . . the *towel boy department*, which is what you asked for as a starting position.

There is one other possibility concerning the fate of your resumés: maybe you didn't have the slightest idea what you were doing, and all the teams ditched them. Maybe all 17,000 people at the game felt the same way you did and they, too, sent in resumés. Maybe *all* the fans at *all* the games in *all* the cities in *all* the sports, sent in resumés, as well.

And you know what? They did.

Your resumé is in a warehouse boxed up with the other thousands that came in recently, and the box is on the *top* shelf *behind* all the other boxes of resumés kept *on file*. Sadly, that's the real truth of what happened to your resumé. You simply are not going to land that plush sports job unless you know the proper procedures.

Each year, tens of millions of young people dream of becoming professional athletes. But let's face it, the odds are better at winning a national lottery than in becoming a star in the big leagues. But wouldn't that front office job with your favorite professional sports franchise be a wonderful alternative? If you can't make it with God-given (or God-lacking) skills as a player, you can toil your way into the dugout or onto the field or court, by way of the administrative duties that each team requires. You *can* be on a professional sports team — if not as a player, then as a staff employee. It would have been nice to have thought of that career possibility years ago while in school, but it's never too late.

In fact, if you know the procedures, and if you know what a team needs, your odds of landing that sports career are better now than ever before. The international community is so bonkers over the sporting industry that career avenues are opening at an astonishing rate worldwide. The sporting industry *needs* you . . . providing you follow the proper channels.

But with all the competition, how do you get your foot in the door of a professional franchise? What positions are available? How do *you* land the job? Whom do you contact? What skills are required? What separates YOU from the competition?

The average sports department director spends an estimated 3.5 seconds browsing resumés. What key words attract his attention for a more thorough reading of YOUR resumé? What prompts him to call YOU for an interview?

This book is your guideline. Follow it, and play ball. Somewhere, somehow, you may find your special niche in the world of sports. The insider's advice should prove invaluable to you. Take it to heart from those who've gone before you and made it into the ranks of the National Basketball Association, the National Football League, Major League Baseball, the National Hockey League and the very lucrative world of minor-league sports.

2

What Exactly Do You Want?

Do you really know what kind of job you want?

If not, it may be a major reason your telephone queries and resumé offerings went unanswered.

It's like playing basketball without a goal — no matter how hard you try, you can't score. Even if you know exactly what you want, the competition you'll face will be tough enough. Don't add to the difficulty by not knowing the rules of the game. How do you expect to land a dream job with your favorite team if you don't know what your dream job is, or what positions exist in the sporting industry?

It is no exaggeration to say that one-half of the resumés received in front offices of sports franchises around the country are accompanied by cover letters that say something to this effect: "I'll take any position I can get. I just love sports."

Can you see a problem here? Since it probably is not addressed to anyone or any department in particular, mail sorters won't know who should get the letter. It will probably sit in the stack of miscellaneous mail that doesn't seem to go anywhere. The last chapter of this book includes a full directory of sports, teams, names and positions. You won't find a single job title that reads, "Director of Anything." Nor will you find, "Director of Towel Boys."

You may find an employee who seems to be the "Director of *Everything*," especially in the minor leagues where employees perform multiple jobs. But you will never, ever be hired by a "Director of People Who've Loved Basketball Since They Were Kids."

Although this is said with tongue-in-cheek, you must understand that half of all resumés submitted to professional teams literally read in such a manner.

BONUS HINT:
Know exactly what you want.

To better understand how failing to define goals can hurt the chances of landing a job, try the following exercise. Let's say you dial the team of your choice, hoping to get an interview for employment for "any position." It doesn't matter what the job is. You'll do anything because you just love these guys. They're your favorites.

Now pretend YOU are the receptionist (who, by the way, has five calls on hold while trying to understand what exactly it is you want). Quickly now, how would you respond to someone who said that to you? You would probably answer with, "Well, do you have a specific person you'd like to speak to?"

"No, I just want anything."

"Do you know what department?"

"Towel boy, or maybe the department in charge of the guy who sits under the basket during the game."

It's amazing how much sense this makes if you can put yourself into that staff employee's predicament. How can *anyone* help you if you don't know what you want yourself? Carrying this simple scenario a bit further, you could have said to the receptionist (assuming that was the

BONUS HINT:
Know exactly with whom to speak.

exact position you wanted), "I bet you get a lot of phone calls, don't you?"

16

"Oh, you have no idea."

"Well, who would I talk to about assisting you?"

"Bless you . . . let me connect you with Mrs. Doe, my supervisor."

> **BONUS HINT:**
> *Find out why she is NOT hiring.*

Get the picture? You've spoken with a staff employee and built a quick rapport by identifying a specific position with a specific need and the correct person with whom to speak. When the office manager gets on the phone you already know half the situation. You've managed to skip all the resumé stuff and jump right to the top.

Unfortunately, you don't know the other half of the situation. Of course she agrees that they could use extra help. But most fans assume everyone in a professional sports organization makes millions of dollars and that there is no such thing as a budget. Nothing could be farther from the truth. Budgets are tightly planned during the off-season and there is little leeway for adding extra staff during a season. Right now, you are told, there is absolutely no money in the budget for hiring assistants.

No problem. You are simply looking for part-time work. You don't need or want full-time pay and benefits.

"We can't even afford part-time help right now. I'd like to hire somebody, but we just don't have room in the budget at this time."

> **BONUS HINT:**
> *Offer a solution that can't be refused.*

No problem. "Just pay me whatever you can afford."

More often than not, the next sound coming out the mouths of office managers, department directors, vice presidents, general managers or owners, will be a hearty laugh, followed with the half-joking words, "We can't afford to pay anything right now."

"OK, that's fair enough. Can I get an interview with you tomorrow about working as an unpaid intern? I'm qualified."

Nice try but no cigar. The office manager has not even considered an intern at this point and can't jump right in without seriously deliberating the possibilities. But the seed is planted and the office manager wonders how it would be if she DID have an intern someday. But not now.

You're not finished. Write a THANK-YOU LETTER to both the receptionist and the office manager in appreciation of their time and helpful advice. You have not yet sent a resumé, only a thank-you letter. Resumés get sent to the warehouse. Thank-you letters get stuffed into the office manager's desk drawer for future reference. She doesn't usually get "Thank-You" letters. She mostly gets requests for free tickets, or for an old uniform from one of the players to be auctioned off for some charity. She gets complaints from disgruntled fans because she was the reason the star player missed that foul shot with time running out to lose the game. But she seldom gets "Thank-You" letters. Your letter might even get tacked onto the cork bulletin board above her desk.

In a month, you call back and say hello to the receptionist and ask if she's still busy. Of course, she is. You ask to be transferred to the office manager. You ask if you can come in for an interview for an unpaid intern.

"OK. How about to-morrow morning?"

Holy Cow, sports fan! You just became an intern

> **BONUS HINT:**
> *Keep in touch. Renew your offer.*

at the position you wanted! And when teams are ready to hire employees for paid, full-time positions they generally take someone who is already there performing the work in a satisfactory manner.

There is no room for error in the highly competitive show time called sports. Experience weighs heavily — GET IT! Even without pay, if necessary. It will eventually pay off, so do it.

But your father said you'd be stupid to work for free. They are just taking advantage of you. He never heard of such a thing. Look at the millions they pay the players. They could at least pay you a couple of thousand a week. Why, way back when he was growing up he at least got paid a nickel an hour. It was hard work, but at least nobody worked for free.

Don't listen. Take the job. Do it. If you refuse there will be three people interviewing for the job the very next day. Your window of opportunity will have slammed in your face. Remember -- if you don't do it, someone else will.

You may not be making a salary at this point but you are sitting under the basket during the Big Game. You don't have money for a hot dog and soda, but you eat a free pregame meal with the rest of the staff and visiting coaches. You may not have money for a ticket to the game, but you have two season tickets in your desk as a benefit. Suddenly you become reacquainted with about 200 friends and cousins who suddenly pop in from who-knows-where wondering how you've been and how badly they feel that they haven't kept in touch over the years. So you let them take turns using your tickets in the staff section, lower level. You won't need them because you'll be down on the court.

Egads! Your friends can't believe it. As a matter of fact, *they'd* like to work for their favorite team, too. They're thinking about calling the front office tomorrow and asking for a job. They don't care what position it is — even a towel boy. They just love basketball.

Do you get the picture now? Do you understand? If you do, you are well on your way to an exciting career in sports.

Just What is Available?

To help you find out what you want, here is a list of several positions and a brief description of each. When you find a job description that seems to pique your career interests, explore every piece of information available about that specific position. To gain in-depth knowledge about the position, you can:

- ◆ Check the local library.
- ◆ Enroll in a college course such as sports management or administration (check the college catalog for course offerings).
- ◆ Write to the specific team for a job description.
- ◆ Ask the appropriate director for an "Information-only" interview.
- ◆ Talk to a person who has a similar job to the one you want. The person probably isn't asked often about his job and is usually more than happy to give helpful answers if you arrange a time to call back.

Although titles, responsibilities and pay vary drastically, most professional teams have similar levels of occupations. Here are some of the typical levels:

OWNER

No application necessary. If you have enough money, you can become a team owner, and once you own a team, you don't have to worry about getting a job with it.

EXECUTIVE POSITIONS

No team will have all of the following positions. Depending on how active the owner is, there may be two or three executive positions available. Today, most executive positions in all four professional sports leagues are filled by former players or coaches, lawyers, people directly connected to the owners' other business interests or the owners' family.

- ◆ President — Runs all aspects of the team, both the business side and player/coach side.
- ◆ General Manager -- Sometimes the same as president, but usually just oversees the player/coach side of the organization.
- ◆ Chief Executive Officer (CEO) — The same as president.
- ◆ Chief Operating Officer (COO) — Usually one step below the CEO but runs the day-to-day operations of a team.
- ◆ Chairman — If the owner wants to divest power, there may be a board of directors. If so, the board is usually responsible for hiring or firing the president or general manager. The chairman would rarely get involved in day-to-day affairs.
- ◆ General Counsel — Depending on the ownership structure, an attorney may be part of the board or executive positions. Some teams will have counsel on a retainer and employ the services on a part-time basis. Whichever setup is used, an attorney is part of the structure in some way.

UPPER MANAGEMENT

Upper management personnel usually have "Vice President" in their titles. VPs come in all shapes: Executive VP, Senior VP, VP of Operations, VP of Administration, VP of Marketing, Sales, Broadcasting, Public Relations, Communications and every other possible department.

The key to determining Upper Management is to see how many VP's there are. If there are two or three, then they are the ones who oversee all or several of the departments within an organization. If there are more than two or three VPs, then the team probably has been rewarding good employees with a title change rather than a pay raise. If that's the case, then look to see if one or two are differentiated by the addition of "Executive" or "Senior."

Heads of the finance department usually are referred to as Chief Financial Officer (CFO) and have a status equal to a vice president.

VP's usually have been involved in the industry for 10-20 years and have developed a diverse background enabling them to oversee many areas. Very few VP's emerge from outside the sports or entertainment industries. Most have been directors for one or more teams, many in more than one department.

MANAGEMENT

The directors, managers and coordinators (and in some cases, vice presidents) are part of the management team. These people do the day-to-day work and head the staffs of various departments. Most of these departments will have entry-level positions and many will employ interns in some capacity during the season. Nearly all have a secretary and/or administrative assistant.

Department names can vary, but most teams will have most of these under some heading:

- ♦ Sales — Could be ticket sales or advertising sales, but someone heading the sales department usually oversees both areas.
- ♦ Ticket Sales/Season Ticket Sales — Usually the person directly responsible for the selling of tickets. Coordinates the efforts of a sales staff which might include a telemarketing group.
- ♦ Group Sales — May be part of Ticket Sales responsibilities. Big in baseball, but rarely needed in football.
- ♦ Ticket Manager — The actual duties of assigning, printing and distributing tickets may fall on the shoulders of

the Ticket Sales Department, but many times a different director will be responsible for the non-selling areas.

♦ Sponsorship Sales/Advertising Sales/Corporate Sales — Sells advertising within the team's radio and TV broadcasts. Will probably also sell other forms of advertising: programs, signage and promotions.

♦ Public Relations/Media Relations/Publicity — Deals directly with the media. Provides information to the media and supervises the press box.

♦ Community Relations/Public Affairs — The liaison with the general public. It fields requests for speakers, autographs, donations, etc. May oversee a team foundation although foundations can be run as separate entities.

♦ Advertising — Unlike Advertising Sales, the Advertising Department buys ads to try to sell tickets or merchandise. It will do the work in-house or contract with an advertising agency.

♦ Broadcast — Oversees getting broadcasts of the games on the air. May also be responsible for the announcers or video needs of a team.

♦ Special Events/Promotions — Coordinates giveaways at games or plans special activities either at the game or away from the stadium.

♦ Merchandising — Handles team sales of T-shirts, hats and other paraphernalia. May also oversee an entire novelty store within the arena or at a local mall.

♦ Game Operations/In-Game Entertainment — Produces the show within the game. Oversees the video screen, scoreboard, music during time-outs, dancers and anthems.

♦ Marketing — A combination of some or all of the above. Sometimes a sliver of the operations; at other times it may entail the entire marketing plan.

♦ Publications/Art/Creative — A luxury for some teams. A whole department may be responsible for putting out printed materials. It may also be responsible for some or all of the advertising.

♦ Controller — Oversees the accounting areas.

♦ Human Resources — Not every team has a separate department, but most teams need a full-time coordinator.

♦ Computer Services/Management Information Systems —
Oversees the computer needs of the company.

TEAM RELATED

Teams also have employees who work directly with the players
and coaches. They may or may not be active in the actual front
office, but there are a number of jobs available to people with specific experience.

♦ Team Doctors — Usually on a retainer to oversee the medical problems of players.

♦ Trainer — In charge of day-to-day health and medical
needs. Will identify and treat minor injuries and discuss
serious ailments with the team doctor.

♦ Equipment Manager/Locker Room Attendant — Handles
team equipment (bats, balls, padding, etc.), and uniforms.
Runs and cleans locker room areas.

♦ Traveling Secretary —A separate job in baseball, but usually part of the trainer's job in other sports. Arranges and
coordinates team's travel plans.

♦ Scout — Watches games in person or on video tape and
looks for potential players or the players of other teams.

♦ Video Coordinator — Gathers video tape of own team, future opponents or players to aid scouts or coaches.

♦ Strength Coach — Oversees the physical fitness of the players, both during the season and off-season.

♦ Personnel Director — Helps determine which players will
be signed. Usually oversees the scouting department.

♦ Minor-League Director/Director of Youth Hockey — Oversees the minor-league teams and development of the
younger players.

♦ Coach/Manager — Teaches skills and decides on strategy.

MISCELLANEOUS

There are many other positions on every team. Besides the ob-
vious assistants to various department heads, there are many jobs
that may or may not require a knowledge of sports. Some are full-
time, others part-time.

♦ Announcers — Play-by-play and color announcers for radio or TV broadcasts.

- Mascot — Depending on the costume, gymnasts may or may not have an advantage.
- Dancers/Ball Girls — May only be part-time, but many dance teams have a full-time choreographer.
- Statistics Crew/Press Room Attendants/Chain Gangs — Part-time, game-day workers to help in the press box or the game officials.
- Team Photographer — Usually part-time, but every team has a need for still photos. Many have a full-time video staff.
- Foreign Relations — Many teams in the South have needs for Hispanic relations which may include sales, public relations or broadcast positions.
- Alumni Coordinators — Keep track of former players and coaches.
- Accountants/Bookkeepers/Payroll Clerks — Every team has bills to pay, checks to cash and salaries to pay.
- Store Clerks/Inventory Control — With many teams now having their own stores, there are a lot of positions open for clerks.
- Administrative Assistants/Secretaries — A great place to get a foot in the door. There is often a lot of turnover in these positions.
- Receptionist — Someone has to answer the telephone, but with the creation of automated attendants and voice mail, the position may be obsolete in a few years.

ARENA/STADIUM PERSONNEL

An area of sports employment that is often overlooked is working directly for the arena or stadium. There are many full- and part-time positions available. If the team actually owns or operates the building, it can be a nice stepping stone to working with the team or a great career in itself.

- Management/Operations — Oversees all stadium operations.
- P.A. Announcer — "Now batting . . ."
- Organist — In many buildings they are as popular and famous as some players.

- Ticket Taker/Usher — Helping with crowd control is a great way to network with the employees of the team who eventually will be doing the hiring.

- Concession Stand Worker/Restaurant Help — See above.

- Scoreboard Operator — Depending on the size and technology, it may take three or four people to operate one scoreboard.

- Video Board Operator — Replay screens require a complete in-house broadcast production of the game. That may require 8-10 people, including one or two full-time.

- Ground Crew/Zamboni Driver — Only non-players or officials to walk on the field or ice during a game.

- Suite Relations/Hosts/Hospitality — With the advent of luxury boxes and suites came the lucrative job of hosting. Even if it doesn't get you a job with a team, it might allow you to network with important people in other industries.

- Box Office — Selling tickets out of the box office is a great way to garner a full-time ticket sales job with any team.

- Security — May get you behind the scenes, but may also be one of the few jobs where you can be injured.

- Parking — Could be a first step to networking or a lucrative career if you own a big garage adjacent to the stadium.

- Novelties — A surefire way to show the merchandise director your sales abilities.

- First Aid — If you desire to be a trainer, good experience and exposure.

Whew! That's a lot of positions. And the industry as a whole offers hundreds, perhaps thousands more than those contained in the listings above. Before reading this book, did you have any idea of the opportunities available within a single franchise? Don't feel badly if you were previously in the dark. Now, you know. You've just narrowed your competition by a million or two. Don't relax, however. You still need to generate a specific "Game Plan" for landing that job.

First and foremost, determine which job you so desperately want to land. If you have no idea at this time, study the list above, and go to several local sporting events with the idea of observing positions in which you have an interest instead of concentrating only on the game.

After the game, approach that person. Depending upon the position (you won't have access to the coach, etc.), the employee will be happy to answer a quick question or two, and probably give you a card to call him during the day hours at the office. Remember, you are a paying customer as long as you are at the game, and it's the employee's job

> **BONUS HINT:**
> *Once you get a name, never forget it. Send a Thank-You letter.*

to be friendly and courteous (to a point that you are not interfering with his duties). So why not walk down to the court and talk to that guy sitting under the basket?

There are many plans of attack an individual can use in job seeking, and only you can decide what works best in your situation.

PLAN "A"

Without a doubt, this is the best of all the job-hunting plans. Without hesitation, simply and boldly march into the general manager's office without an appointment. Don't waste your time calling. Don't waste your time with the secretary. Just walk on in. HOWEVER, the first words out of your mouth better truthfully be, "Hi, Uncle Bob. Where should I start?"

Ah-ha! The old "It's Not WHAT You Know, It's WHO You Know" ploy. Yes. It's true. "Who you know" is vital. However, you can get around that. You'll learn how in a later chapter. For now, let's pretend that Uncle Bob isn't hiring his nephew and that he wants someone with real qualifications. On to Plan "B."

PLAN "B"

Not as good as PLAN "A," but effective, nonetheless. PLAN "B" is perhaps the most difficult of all the plans you'll ever concoct, but worth every moment of the time you put into developing this career guidance blueprint.

Not meaning to sound discouraging, but PLAN "B" is so diffi-cult to perfect that most would-be sports career hopefuls save it as a last resort, or more often than not, don't even attempt it. Perhaps it should more aptly be dubbed, "PLAN Z" or maybe even "PLAN ZZ." Nonetheless, here goes at a wild attempt to explain a perfect PLAN "B."

1. Go to a quiet room, such as your own bedroom, the base-ment, if you have one, or the local library in the middle of the week during summer vacation when nobody is using it. Get somewhere, anywhere, where you can concentrate.

2. Take out a piece of paper and a pencil (a pen will be fine).

3. Write down exactly what you want. That's it.

Oh, dear God, no! Not THAT! Anything but THAT! Don't make me figure out what I want to do. It's much easier to say, "I'll do anything."

Those earlier examples were cute, but doesn't a team really — I mean REALLY — take into consideration that I've played football all my life? I played college ball, for crying out loud. They scouted one of the guys on my team. They probably remember Willie Williamson — nicknamed "Bear." I played right behind him, and would have made it professionally as a player had I not blown out my knee. Or, was it an elbow? No, it was politics, that's right. Now I remember. The coach liked Bear best, even though I was better.

> **BONUS HINT:**
>
> *It is essential to know what you want, and to have a plan for achieving that goal.*

Anyway, that has to count for something, doesn't it, that I've loved the game all my life?

NO!

Actually, you need TWO plans: (1) a long-range plan, in which you select your ultimate dream job, and; (2) a short-range plan to determine which entry-level positions might point you in the right direction to achieve your long-term goal.

It is important to be truthful with yourself. You can try to fool your friends and relatives with your lofty, somewhat dreamy, ca-reer plans, in which you boast that you will someday own a sports franchise, or will be general manager, coach, or whatever. If that is what you truly want, and if that is something you can honestly say you will someday be qualified for after following a sensible career plan, then go for it. Otherwise, quit kidding yourself, and find something that would really be suitable for you.

Know your strengths, but also know your weaknesses. If you have never played football professionally, you will probably never be qualified for a position as head scout. Although there have been exceptions, those windows of opportunities are growing smaller every day. That is a position, however, where you might try the

> **BONUS HINT:**
> *Give yourself a fighting chance by keeping your goals realistic. Be honest with yourself, but don't sell yourself short, either.*

minor leagues, especially in the lower levels with a new team as an independent contractor (they have several names given for these positions). Miracles sometimes happen. If what you want to be is a scout, then by all means, develop your career plan and go for it.

PLAN C

This plan of attack should be reserved as a last resort, but one that could still be quite effective for getting your foot in the door of a professional franchise. You've tried getting a job in your main area of interest and didn't get anywhere. You tried the secondary, entry-level positions that would have led you in the proper direction on your long-term career path. You hit nothing but brick walls there, too.

Now you are faced with the dilemma of either continuing your plan, which seems to be going nowhere (YES! Do continue), or sadly let your dreams of a sporting career fade as you get a job in the local department store and try to move up its ladder. Again, if that is what you want, go for it. But don't let that sporting career dream fade.

Take a good look at that job descriptions list again. You've tried the "Department Directors" route and got nowhere. You tried the "Assistants" positions and got shown the door without ever being called back. Look again at the Jobs List. Go to a baseball game, or a hockey game, etc. Look at ALL the people who seem to be working there in some capacity or another.

Were you truthful with yourself? Do you seriously WANT a career in sports? Would you truly be willing to take ANY position? You must understand that the positions you applied for were probably tried as well by hundreds or more of others every bit as hopeful as you.

How many people do you suppose apply for parking lot attendant? Not so many. How many apply for parking security, or concessions vendors? Not enough to keep you from ever getting your foot in the door if you keep at it. The fact is, the higher the position — the more glamorous the profile — the stiffer the competition. Swallow your pride and rethink what you first said, that you'd be willing to take any job.

Question: Who is one person guaranteed to meet every athlete on the team?

Answer: The parking attendant.

Question: Who is one person guaranteed to meet the owner, every executive officer, every department director and every merchandise store clerk?

Answer: The parking lot attendant.

The position of parking attendant is used only as an example. There are many positions — low in nature compared to your lofty goals, and without glamour to impress your friends — that will get you in the door in relatively short time. Chances are, they won't hire you right away for these positions, either. However, the competition is small, and the turnover high. Sooner or later, you'll get that call for a personal interview for one of the lower-profile positions.

When you start work, do the best job they've ever had done. Be friendly and make acquaintances with EVERYONE.

Continue PLAN B, only this time, you can put on your cover letter that you work in concessions for the team, or in the parking garage of the arena, or whatever.

Best of all . . . you get to HAND-DELIVER your resumés.

3

A Gold Mine of Insider Advice

If you want to mine gold, the only way is to go inside the mine and get it. If you want a sports career, then here is your gold mine of advice, taken from within the ranks of the National Basketball Association, the National Football League, Major League Baseball and the National Hockey League.

A virtual treasure chest of knowledge, these staff members tell you such vital information as how they first got into their respective leagues, how they moved up the ladders to their present day status, how you should go about getting your start in the sports industry today, and other exciting details that will no doubt help pave the way down your career path.

Take to heart every word they say. They are telling you these specifics for a reason, even if you don't presently understand their logic the first time through. This is one list you'll want to read, reread, and refer to often.

> **BONUS HINT:**
>
> *Add these names to the network of sports personnel that you "know."*

Also, try to find some common ground in what all of them are saying. If you see a related theme in many of them, take note, and put that very same theme in your repertoire of sports career necessities.

CAUTION:

People in sports move from one team to the next with relative ease. Always place a quick call to the reception-ist and ask if so-and-so still works there and is still the director of such-and-such. Try to avoid blindly writing to someone who is no longer with the franchise.

JIM BRYLEWSKI
Detroit Tigers (MLB)
Marketing Coordinator

Passed out items at the gate for the Tigers for two years before getting an internship.

I tell people going for their first job in sports to not worry about what the job is or how much it pays. Those should be the last concerns if they really want a job in the business. They have to be willing to do anything for nothing or close to nothing.

I got a job with the Tigers in 1990. I was going to school at Michigan State. The Tigers started a pretty aggressive promotional program and I showed up on a Saturday morning and offered to hand out stuff at the gate. I did that for a couple of summers and that led to an internship and the position I'm currently in.

As marketing coordinator, I'm responsible for all the game entertainment, the Jumbrotron, features, on-field ceremonies, anthem singers, music and promotional items.

I think sports administration degrees are a little over-rated. I have an advertising degree. My boss has a law degree. The college majors are pretty varied here with the Tigers. The business is so specialized and each team operates differently. Besides, if you get a sports admin-istration degree and you don't get a job with a team, where do you go from there?

MARY BURNS
Colorado Rockies (MLB)
Director of Management Information Systems

Got her first job in sports while wearing shorts and a T-shirt by asking for an autographed ball.

A long time ago, I walked into the major-league baseball commissioner's office, right off the beach in shorts and a T-shirt, and got an autographed ball. The director of data processing happened to need someone and I just happened to have graduated, so for me, it was truly a case of being in the right place at the right time. I worked there for five years and then moved to Colorado. I heard that a new team was coming and started calling and sending my resume to the ownership group. I got an interview and a job.

The key is to get out and network as much as you can. You have to be persistent. Take advantage of every opportunity. Go to events where someone from a team's front office might be speaking or where a team might be represented. Look for someone in a suit, or a dress and heels, and start talking with them. I've hired people as interns who just walked up to me at an event and impressed me. People should also look at a sports team as a big business and understand that there is a finance department, a legal department and every other department that you find at all big businesses. Don't assume that the only jobs are sports marketing jobs. There are lots of other ones.

JOE CHARD
Seattle Mariners (MLB)
Director of Community Relations

Was working full time with a not-for-profit foundation when the opportunity to work for the Mariners arose five years ago.

I got my start in sports through a non-profit. I was the executive director of the Cystic Fibrosis Foundation for the state of Washington. We got involved in the "65 Roses" program with the local sports teams, did golf outings and a lot of sports-oriented promotions. Our philosophy was to get a hook and sports was our hook. We found that people bought into it and sponsors bought into it. I think people started looking around and saw how well the charities were doing and that's how I ended up with the Mariners.

I tell those who are trying to get into sports to get an internship, but it doesn't have to be with a sports team. Look beyond sports franchises to related fields, like a radio affiliate or a local company that sponsors a lot of sporting events. Sometimes organizations offer internships to work on a specific program for the summer. I also encourage people to volunteer for non-profits that are involved in sports. I think internships of some kind are the best way to go. Most of the people at the Mariners started out as an intern somewhere.

BILL CONNELLY
Cincinnati Bengals (NFL)
Business Manager

An 18-year career with the Bengals began with a summer stint as a student trainer.

I was a student trainer at Ohio State University and the trainer of the Bengals came to our spring practice one day looking for a part-time helper during training camp. I got the job, but a year later when I graduated, the Bengals did not have a full-time assistant trainer. But they did help me get a job with the Stingers in the World Hockey Association. I worked there for 2½ years until the WHA merged with the NHL. When the Stingers became a minor-league team, I walked next door to the Coliseum and told Coach Brown that I was available. He told me, "We'll hire you, effective tomorrow." They made me a full-time assistant trainer. And four years later, I became business manager.

I tell people interested in getting into sports two things:

1) Do whatever you have to do to get your foot in the door.

2) It's still a matter of being in the right place at the right time.

It typically becomes who you know. I'm not a big fan of letters. I don't think resumés and letters get the job done. If an exhibition game comes to town, volunteer to do something. Be there so you can become known and make contacts.

CHUCK DOUGLAS
Washington Bullets (NBA)
Assistant General Manager

Basically created his own job with the Bullets and has worked his way up in a world usually reserved for former players or coaches.

If you want to get involved in the area of scouting, there's no one way of going about it. There are former NBA players and former NBA coaches, as well as former head college coaches. If that's the case, then your notoriety might get you a job. But for everyone else, you have to find another way. I didn't plan it. I just wanted to get into the front office and then I kind of fell into the player personnel side.

I was a sports administration major at the University of Maryland and did three or four internships while I was an undergraduate. The Bullets offered me a temporary position in the media relations department, primarily to take care of all the requests for Manute Bol, who the Bullets had just drafted. At the end of that season my job was over, but they needed someone to edit video tapes for the upcoming college draft. I did that and then edited their pro tapes that fall. I didn't have a basketball background, but I sat down with the coaches and picked up the terminology. I then started going out and watching games in person and one thing led to another. The lesson to be learned is that if you work hard and are a team player, they'll find a way to keep you around.

BOB ELLER
Cleveland Browns (NFL)
Director of Operations/Information

Started working for the Baltimore Colts as an intern. Now is director of operations for the Browns.

> *I got my first chance in sports when I was a student at Towson State University. I saw an internship with the Colts posted and went out and applied. I got the position and did very basic office duties. The team then moved from Baltimore to Indianapolis and they offered me a full-time position as assistant PR director. I accepted and within a year I became head of the department when the new PR director didn't work out.*

> *My advice to everyone is that no matter what their background and no matter what it is they want to get into, the one thing they can never do enough of is write. That's a key in any profession. You need to constantly upgrade your communication skills. Once you feel strongly about your abilities, then send out those resumes. Unfortunately, it still comes down to being in the right place at the right time, or who you know.*

> *The openings in this business are few and far between, and normally, people look within the industry to fill positions. So if you don't have the experience, it can be very difficult. But if you are willing to sacrifice some dollars and time, you might be able to gain some experience by helping out part-time on game days or at training camp.*

MOIRA FOY
Chicago White Sox (MLB)
Director of Human Resources

Answered a classified ad in the newspaper to get her job with the White Sox.

> *It's important to know when teams are adding to their staffs. Baseball teams don't typically hire in midseason,*

36

so the summers are bad for anyone looking for a job in baseball.

At the White Sox we are looking to have a diverse staff. We look to people who didn't have a traditional background of working in the SID office or who ushered when they were a kid. We encourage them to go through an internship program with our organization. If we have a staff of eight interns, we try to have eight very different people with different life experiences. We've had very good success with people who are re-entering the work force. It creates a good balance and gets them to learn to work together. We have very few openings for full-time jobs, but when we do have an opening, we do an internal posting first. Except for the highest executive positions, we do most of our hiring internally.

There are exceptions to every rule. I got my job out of the newspaper. We very rarely advertise for a job, only if it is very specialized or requires a high degree of experience, like in human resources.

HARVEY GREENE
Miami Dolphins (NFL)
Director of Media Relations

Has been an award-winning PR director in three sports — the NBA's Cleveland Cavaliers, MLB's New York Yankees and the NFL's Miami Dolphins.

I majored in chemistry at Penn, but went to U-Mass for their graduate sports administration program. While I was there, I got an internship with the Nets through a friend. And I've been involved in sports ever since.

I always tell people that if you don't have any experience, then the only way to get a job in sports is to go through one of the graduate programs in sports administration. They're great at helping you get internships and making a lot of contacts. If you can't get back to school, then you have to volunteer to help out on game days. And don't just set your sights on the major leagues. Work for a tennis tournament, a golf outing or some-

thing else in your area, and hopefully the contacts you make there will help you.

Of the three leagues I've worked in, baseball is a little easier to break in with, only because there are so many more front office positions. In baseball, there's a whole department to run the team's minor leagues. And with 81 home games, baseball teams have larger sales and marketing departments. In football, we have only eight home games, so we don't need a group sales department. Eight games? That's a short home stand in baseball.

ZACK HILL
Philadelphia Flyers (NHL)
Media Relations Manager

After working with the Philadelphia 76ers as PR director, moved across town to do a similar job with the Flyers.

I got an undergraduate degree at West Virginia University and then began working toward a master's degree in sports management there. I sent out all kinds of letters looking for an internship. I wanted to stay close to Philadelphia and wound up getting on with the 76ers. At the end of my internship, the general manager asked me if I wanted to stay on board. I wasn't about to tell him "No, I'm going back to school to finish my master's." I was going to school to get that kind of job, so I put school on hold and took my first job in the club's ticket office.

My advice is to definitely go through an internship program. That's much better than sending out blind resumés. It's not easy getting good internships, though. You have to be persistent. Call or write to the organizations you're interested in and follow up.

To someone who is still in high school and wondering what courses to take in college, it all depends on the area you want to get into. I wanted to get into PR, so I took a lot of photo-journalism, public speaking and writing classes. It's different if you want to go into marketing or promotions or sales.

GREG JAMISON
San Jose Sharks (NHL)
Chief Operating Officer

After spending 13 seasons working for teams in the NBA as a marketing director and VP, moved to the Sharks and the NHL in 1993.

The first thing I tell anyone interested in working in sports is to be willing to relocate. Some people want to stay in their area and that just limits the possibilities. The next thing is the willingness to start at an entry level position. Some people go through internships or summer sales programs. Another possibility is to work part-time for the arena or full-time for a company that interacts with a team. I'm talking about advertising agencies, vendors who call on the arena or team, or maybe a TV or radio station.

I also advise: Don't try to get with a team when it's hot. Go find an organization that is down. There's less competition and it may be in need of some sharp people. And eventually, all teams turn it around. Finally, stay in touch. Do it in a professional way and it will make an impact.

I got my first job in sports with Athletes In Action. You really have to be committed to do that, because you have to raise your own support to get on staff. It gave me valuable on-the-job training in all aspects of the business and opened the doors for a job with the Dallas Mavericks.

CAROL KOLBUS
New Jersey Devils (NHL)
Coordinator of Game Entertainment

Oversees the Devils' game night video, music, mascot, promotions and intermission entertainment. Prior to that, worked in the front office of the International Hockey League.

I had an internship with TicketMaster when I was in

college at Butler University. I was a public and corporate communications major, and in one of my classes they announced all types of internships. My main reason for working with TicketMaster was that I wanted to get into the sports field, and I figured they handle the tickets for all of the sports teams. Right out of school I got a full-time job with TicketMaster and worked with them for about a year. While I was there, I made a good contact with someone at the local hockey team and he recommended me for a job with the International Hockey League office. I worked for the IHL for about a year-and-a-half and then my boss at the time got a job with the Devils. After about three months, he called and offered me the position I now have with the Devils.

I tell everyone who wants to get into sports to do internships. Besides the one I did with TicketMaster, I also did one with the RCA tennis tournament. It's a great way to learn responsibility and learn what really goes on in the sports marketing field. It's also a great way to network. Just start off volunteering any way you can and get to know as many people as you can.

RENE LONGORIA
Indianapolis Colts (NFL)
Director of Sales

Didn't enter sports industry until he was 35, now he heads up broadcast sales and promotions.

I was working in sales for a radio station that carried the games of the Colts, along with the Indiana Pacers, Indianapolis Ice and Indianapolis Indians. I worked on station promotions and a number of other events with the various teams.

I always liked sports, but I never called myself an "avid" fan. When I got my job with the Colts, it was because I knew more about advertising, promotions and corporate marketing through sports, than I did about who the Colts should draft. The Colts had never had anyone walk out of their offices and try to sell associa-

tions with the corporate world, and I happened to be there when they made the decision to do so.

My advice to everyone is to not get too focused on the idea of working for a professional sports team, but focus on the tools of the trade you are getting into. Try everything so you can find out what you are most comfortable dealing with. Some people like retail sales. Some people like to help other people, so they might end up in public relations.

Finally, don't overcommit and underdeliver. If you can't do it, don't say it.

DON MacLACHLAN
Houston Oilers (NFL)
Senior Vice President/Marketing and Broadcasting

Joined the Oilers in 1990 after 12 years at Northwestern University, where he worked in many capacities: assistant AD, golf coach, ticket manager, assistant SID.

I tell everyone that getting a job in professional sports is all a matter of opportunity, breaks and timing. But another important aspect that is often overlooked is that you have to be willing to relocate. That improves your marketability and shows that you can be successful in another marketplace where you don't really know anybody.

To succeed in this business, it all comes down to establishing relationships. It's the strength of those relationships that really solidifies you in your job. And those same relationships come into play when it's time to move on.

I also believe that you have to broaden your experiences. Don't get stuck in just one field. I started out in the SID office, but wound up working in the ticket office and even coached the golf team before I was named an assistant AD. Offer to help out in any area you can get involved in. And get started early. If you don't get into the field early, it's really hard to get into. Most teams are looking for young people to start out at a rather small

41

salary and have them work their way up through the organization.

ANN-MARIE MALARCHUK
Calgary Flames (NHL)
Ticket Manager

A 14-year veteran of the Flames, she began in sports after selling tickets for other entertainment events.

I was with the Calgary Exhibition, where the Flames' building is, working in the ticket office, selling tickets for concerts or whatever else came to town. When the Flames moved in, I started to do tickets for them. They had their own computer files, but I did all the manual work for them. They eventually asked me to come over and work for them full-time and I went.

Now that sports is such a business, you no longer come in to just work for "a team." It's a whole business you are going to work for. At a lot of clubs, there's room to grow and move up in the franchise. For example, if you are interested in marketing, that's an area that has grown by leaps and bounds. At most clubs in the NHL, the marketing departments are getting bigger and bigger. If you get with a team at the right time, you can move up quickly.

I tell people they definitely have to have a good solid background in school and ... know somebody.

How do you get to know somebody?

Find out when the busy time of the year for a team is and then volunteer to help out on a project. A lot of clubs will take on people like that.

JEFF NEWMAN
Toronto Maple Leafs (NHL)
Retail Operations Manager

Joined the Maple Leafs four years ago after working as a retail consultant and running a family-owned business.

Anyone wanting to get into the retail side of sports, first and foremost, needs to have a background in retail sales. They need to understand what retail is all about, be it working in sports or at The Gap. They have to understand that it's dealing with people. That's something that isn't easily taught. Secondly, you have to have an understanding of the marketplace. And then you need to understand the product.

In learning to deal with people, you need to understand the politics that exist, whether you work in a sports organization or for IBM. There are politics and turf wars in offices wherever you go. Everybody wants to protect their domain, be it marketing or merchandising or properties or whatever. And your ability to understand and deal with those politics will determine just how well you can do your job.

I got my job with the Maple Leafs when a new president came on board and made a lot of changes in how the organization operated. One of the areas that needed immediate upgrades was merchandising. My name was forwarded to the right people, and I was lucky enough to get the job.

YOSHI OKAMOTO
New Jersey Nets (NBA)
Director of International Marketing

Only Japanese native working in the front office of a team in the four major sports leagues.

Any business — including sports — that wants to grow, needs to grow globally. If you can speak another language and understand another country's culture, it will be a big advantage. Typical American students only speak English, but if they can learn a foreign language, as well as learn the business customs of a particular country, it could very well lead them to a position with a sports team or any company that does business overseas.

43

I was born and raised in Japan and lived there until I graduated from college. I came to the United States when I was 22 years old and got a job with a minor-league baseball team. I had gained a lot of experience working with the baseball associations in Japan and one day I got a call from a man — half Japanese, half American — who was buying a team and wanted me to help run it. I worked for that Class A team for two years, then moved to a Triple A team in Portland, Ore. Then I got a call from Disney to work for the Mighty Ducks. A year ago I began working for the Nets to try to sell sponsorships to Japanese-based companies with business dealings in the New York / New Jersey area.

BLAKE PAYNE
Charlotte Hornets (NBA)
Mascot Coordinator/Office Assistant

Walked in cold to get an internship, then parlayed that into a full-time position.

I got an internship with the Triple A baseball team in Charlotte by walking in cold. I was home from college for Christmas vacation and had my suit and my resume. I think I was the first person to come in and ask about the following season, so I got an interview. I was pretty aggressive and didn't let up. I followed the interview with some telephone calls and got the job.

That team has the same owner as the Hornets, so that sort of led me to knowing about a position there. I got a good recommendation. Now I coordinate all of our mascot's activities. But I've never gone on an appearance for him. I wouldn't be able to, because my feet are too big for the suit!

I was a sports management major in college, but if I had it to do again, I think I'd concentrate on a major more specific to the area I'd want to go into. The sports management major covers some things other majors don't, but I don't think it's necessary to get a job. If you want to go into sales, then a business major is probably better. If you want to go into community relations, like I'm in, I think public relations would be a better major.

HARVEY POLLACK
Philadelphia 76ers (NBA)
Director of Statistical Information

Began working in pro sports in 1946 and will celebrate his 50th year in the NBA during the 1995-96 season.

> *Right after World War II, I took a job as a sports reporter in Philadelphia making $28 a week. I had kept statistics in college and kept doing it on the side, first for Temple football, then for the area college basketball teams. The NBA was formed in 1946, and they were looking for someone to keep statistics. I got the job and that eventually led to working with the Philadelphia Warriors full-time. In the early days, there were only four people in the entire front office. Now there are what, 50 or 60? And the league office, there were six people, including a secretary. Now they must have 600. There are a lot more opportunities today.*

> *My advice to people trying to get one of those jobs is: Get some experience. A college degree alone doesn't mean much. Whether it's a job in an office or statistics or whatever, nothing replaces experience. People also need to realize that it isn't a 9-to-5 job. I end up working as much at home as I do in the office.*

> *I'm happy to say that my son also keeps statistics and my grandson, who is 22, is helping me out now, too. But I plan to retire by the time he has a son, so don't be looking for a four-generation stat crew.*

BILL ROBERTSON
Mighty Ducks of Anaheim (NHL)
Director of Public Relations

After gaining experience with the expansion Minnesota Timberwolves in the NBA, he moved to another expansion team, the Mighty Ducks of Anaheim in the NHL.

There are five keys to getting a job in sports. The first is using common sense. The second is attention to detail. The third is proactive vs. reactive. The fourth is excellent communication skills, both orally and written. And the fifth is have fun at what you do.

Everyone interested in getting a job in professional sports, regardless of their age or experience, has to network with people in the industry. Without doing that, it's very difficult. You have to put yourself in situations where you are face-to-face with the people you want to network with. It might be at charity events or other community functions. It's the only way you are going to get them.

I worked five or six different part-time jobs in sports before I found anything full-time. I was interested in PR, so I worked in radio, television, newspapers and public relations. That was my selling point. I knew what each of the media wanted and needed. They're not all the same.

I used all the connections and people I knew to get a job with the Timberwolves. I networked for two years in advance of Minnesota even being granted a franchise.

WENDY SOMMERS
Indiana Pacers (NBA)
Advertising Director

Worked her way up from receptionist to head of an award-winning advertising department.

I went through an employment agency to find a job. I wasn't specific with the agency, other than I told them I wanted a job that had some excitement to it. They sent me to the Pacers to interview as the receptionist. Having graduated from college, I wasn't looking to make a career out of being a receptionist, but I was excited about the possibility of working for a professional sports team.

After five months, there was an opening for the coaches' secretary and I got that job. Then two years later, I became the administrative assistant to the general manager. After four years there, I got promoted to director of merchandise and advertising.

The best advice I can give anyone is to do research and know what kinds of jobs exist with a team. Then try to get to know as many people within the organization as you can. If an opening does come up, be willing to take anything to get started. Let them know that even if you are overqualified for a particular position, you are more than willing to take it and you'll stick with it as long as necessary. Once you begin working for a team, you'll probably find any job "fun" and want to stay with the organization in any capacity. And if you remain patient and work hard, you'll be in a good position to get promoted.

DIANE STACK
Cleveland Indians (MLB)
Coordinator of Season/Group Sales

Was working as a waitress in a Chinese restaurant when she got a job with the Indians through an employment agency.

Many people begin as interns. The ones that do a great job seem to get offered a full-time position with the team.

I was lucky. I was waiting tables at a Chinese restaurant for 10 years. I didn't go to college until I was in my late 20s. A couple of months after I graduated, I went to an employment firm and they sent me on an interview with the Indians. I had a job two days later. I actually interviewed for an administrative assistant job, but after the interview, they offered me the position of coordinator of sales.

When we moved into our new ballpark, we got very "corporate." Now when people send in resumés and an application we ask them to fill out, we pass around the applications to each department depending on the person's background. A lot of people are called in for interviews. Most of the people in sales are hired full-time after working in our telemarketing division.

Not too many people here have degrees in sports. My degree is in communications, and I can't imagine having a more fun or exciting job.

JOE TAIT
Cleveland Cavaliers (NBA)
Vice President of Broadcasting

Longtime announcer has done a variety of sports at every level, including the Cavs in the NBA and Indians in MLB.

To be a broadcaster, there are three keys. First, you have to have some talent, an ability to describe what you are seeing. Second, you have to go to work in a small market and perfect your skills. You have to get some experience so that no matter what comes up, you'll be able to cope with it. And third, now more than ever, you have to develop contacts. This is a real people business. You have to know people and develop good relationships with people who can help you. The competition is fierce. It seems as if every college has a broadcast department dumping people into the market place by the thousands.

My first job in radio was as a janitor at a 1,000-watt daytime station in Illinois. By the time I left that station five years later, I was the operations manager and had done everything at the station except for chief engineer. But it wasn't until later, in 1970, when I got into professional sports. I had given up sports play-by-play and was managing a station in Terre Haute, Ind. I had been friends with Bill Fitch, who wound up becoming head coach of the Cavs. It was my contact with him that was instrumental in getting the job. And that has led to many other opportunities along the way.

DOUG WARD
California Angels (MLB)
Publications Manager

Has worked for teams in three leagues: the Rams in the NFL, the Timberwolves in the NBA and now the Angels in MLB.

Get an internship. Call all the teams and tell them you're willing to work for nothing. Tell them you are hungry and want to work. That's what I did and it worked for me. I did an internship with the Angels and there are probably another six people who are full time who did it the same way. The Angels do a huge cattle call in January or February and whittle that down until they wind up with about 10 interns a summer in a variety of departments. I've been with the Angels for four years now. I did the internship in '85, then went to work for the Rams and the Timberwolves full time before returning to the Angels.

The easiest way to get an internship is to have an in. Then use it and abuse it. If you don't know anyone, call and tell them you'll be in the neighborhood and can you stop in for a few minutes.

Based on my experiences, baseball might be the easiest league to get an internship with. The internship gives you an opportunity to establish a reputation and let's you know when there's a full-time job opening up.

MINOR LEAGUES

Here is some additional insider's advice from within the ranks of some top minor-league franchises. Minor-league sports could prove vital to your career plans. You may want to give some thoughtful consideration here, because it is a viable career path that may offer more than you realize.

It used to be that sports personnel treated the minor leagues as a stepping stone to the big leagues, much the same way the athletes hoped to advance from one level to the next. However, that has changed very much. The economic stability of minor-league sports has demonstrated over the years that a solid franchise can offer a lifetime career within its own rank-and-file. Don't overlook the minor leagues as a career move.

Even as this book goes to press, another large professional league in the minors has begun in the Midwest. Owners of major-league franchises are realizing the economic virtues of owning minor-league franchises and are adding minor-league teams to their ownership portfolios.

Minor-league sports offers a unique touch of glamour, in that you get to meet athletes on their way up to the big leagues, or those who've come down from the big leagues for one reason or another, be it age, injury rehabilitation or skills enhancements. Athletes on their way up are usually quite humble, and appreciate your interest in them. They tend to remember you when they make it to the top, especially if you've stuck by them during their slumping periods. Many employee-athlete friendships have developed in this manner, which is a nice side benefit to a minor-league career.

A minor-league team can often be the most exciting show in town, giving you an extra sense of pride. Be advised to take a long, hard look at your career options in the minors. A minor-league career can have big-time rewards.

RAY COMPTON

Former sportswriter now is co-owner of a minor-league baseball team, a Continental Basketball Association team, a Canadian Football League franchise and 10 minor-league hockey teams.

People who work in the minor leagues are usually less specialized and everyone has to be willing to sell. That's good training. You can learn more about the entire system and that might qualify you to move up the ranks a little quicker. If you stick with it at the minorleague level, there's a very good chance you can wind up as a general manager, running an entire organization. At a major-league team, you can get pigeon-holed and maybe not get promoted as quickly or find the niche you're most comfortable in.

I'm very partial to hiring people who were interns. It gets your foot in the door and gives you a leg up on those people that have no experience at all. But don't be choosy about the type of internship you have. Just get on the merry-go-'round and don't worry about the color of the horse. Look at that internship as the biggest opportunity you'll have to get into professional sports. If it means working 80 hours a week, work 80 hours a week. Be enthusiastic and show a willingness to learn. If you do that, you have a reasonable chance of getting a job at some point.

DAVID PAITSON

Currently president of the Columbus Chill in the American Hockey League. He also has worked for NBA and minor-league baseball teams.

It may be slightly easier to get a job with a minor-league team than a major-league team simply because there are probably less people going after the available jobs. Plus, there are a lot more minor-league teams and leagues than there are major-league teams. Yet, it still is very competitive.

Another advantage of working for a minor-league team is the diversification of the experiences. The staffs usually are small, and that allows everyone to do a variety of tasks. Unlike a major-league team where jobs are very specific, you are expected to get hands-on experience in a lot of different areas. And everyone is counted on to sell. That's the key. If you can sell tickets, sponsorships or whatever, you're going to have an easier time finding a job.

A sports administration degree is looked upon as a positive, but work experience outweighs education. Be willing to do full-time, non-paid internships. Those go a long way in showing that you are serious about getting into the business. And finally, don't expect a large salary. Everyone has to pay their dues. Sacrifice money in your early years for the possible long-term payoff.

RICH WOLFE

Has served as a marketing consultant for several minor-league baseball, basketball and hockey teams.

My advice for getting a job with a minor-league team is to be relentless. There are so many letters, resumés, tapes and calls that it's difficult to stand out. It's true, but the squeaky wheel gets the most oil. You really have to let the right people know that you want the job. Go into an interview with some creative ideas, like how you can sell more tickets or corporate sponsorships. Younger people generally don't have the experience to be that creative, but even if the ideas aren't that good, it shows that you are thinking and are open to ideas. You also need to show a willingness to work and learn. Too many people just want the glamour of hanging around the players, but you have to show that you are willing to get your hands dirty. Most people aren't prepared to work long enough, hard enough or smart enough.

I get most of my jobs by coming up with an idea. I read something and say, "Boy, could I help that guy there." Sometimes they don't want any help, sometimes they do. The biggest fear is change. It's much easier to keep on doing things the way they've always been done.

On the minor-league level, you'll probably have more responsibility than working for a major-league team. You'll have a quicker return on seeing your work pay off. And you'll probably get involved in a lot more areas which will make you more well rounded as you move up the ladder.

4

Resumé Do's and Don'ts

Assuming that the person to whom you are applying for a position is not "Uncle Bob," you are going to have to show a potential employer that you possess some outstanding qualifications that separate you from the masses. This is generally done with a top-notch, attention-getting resumé that makes your personal charisma leap out at the director and make him want to meet you.

Keep in mind that the purpose of a resumé is to get a personal interview with a decision maker, not derive actual employment based upon the contents of a slip of paper. No resumé has enough swaying power to make a professional sports franchise tell you to come in to work Monday morning. Again, there are exceptions to everything, but speaking in general terms, it won't happen.

Therefore, it is your objective to put forth a resumé of personal experiences and characteristics that would entice a potential employer to pick up the telephone or pass your resumé to his secretary to call on his behalf to schedule an appointment. In this light, your resumé is paramount to landing that personal interview. Your first goal is to literally get your foot in the door. If you don't "Know someone" then you'll have to make your resumé speak on your behalf to separate you from the competition.

Hone your resumé writing skills. Take note, however, that a resumé for a professional sports franchise can be quite different from a resumé you might send to a more general line of business. You'll need to learn a few tricks of the trade.

At this point, you need a basic idea of how a morning begins in the front office of a typical professional sports franchise. This is not a 9-to-5 type of career. On game nights, the employees are required to work at the game in various capacities, and those who don't work are in attendance watching. Therefore, on the day after a game, the employees mill around the office for a few minutes discussing the great win or the unfortunate loss. If the team was on the road, most of the employees come in with bloodshot eyes, having stayed up late to watch the West Coast game. If the team didn't play that evening, then employees still mill about the office discussing scores around the league, or else they open the sports pages and get the latest. Few offices allow the reading of sports on company time, but not only is it tolerated here, it's practically a requirement. In fact, the media relations department scans various publications from around the country, cuts-and-pastes pertinent articles for the photocopy machine, then distributes them to every employee to read. It's the nature of the business, albeit a fun nature.

The first place most staff members visit upon arrival is the lunch room, where the coffee pot is working in overdrive, as well as the bottled spring water dispenser for the several health-conscious employees always found in sports-oriented businesses. If the team has a morning workout, the players often stroll through the office and make conversation.

When the employees get back to their desks, the work is already piled up, either unfinished business from the day before (the stacks of work never diminish), or from new business, including urgent phone messages that must be dealt with immediately. No doubt the phone calls launch the day's work into high gear, and there goes the day. Some careers seem to make clock-watchers out of their employees, but the only clock-watching staff members will do, once the day gets going, is to fret about time running out.

For example, picture yourself in sponsorship sales and promotions. Part of your job is to coordinate the television and radio commercial traffic. You have a game tomorrow and the time slots are all filled, and the team's flagship stations have all the commercials on their systems, ready to go at the given cues, such as timeouts, end-of-quarters, halftime, etc. You've enjoyed your morning chats in the lunch room, but now you've taken your orange juice back to your desk for the phone messages. Nothing urgent, there, either. An easy day lies ahead.

You get your mail that has now been posted. First, you open the big package from the largest beer company in the world, your biggest sponsor who pays megadollars to advertise on BOTH your television AND radio broadcasts, on the entire network of multiple stations, several spots per game, for every game, including preseason, postseason and the coach's show.

OH NO! PANIC CITY!

They've included a tape full of all new commercials and demand that you rotate out all the current ones and replace them with these for tomorrow's game. "THEY CAN'T DO THAT!" you scream to your immediate supervisor. They know that the deadline for commercial changes has long since passed, and that the entire game has already been loaded and set to run. "ARE THEY CRAZY?!"

You place an urgent call to the television flagship station as well as to the radio flagship. Their program director screams, "THEY WHAT?!!!" While you listen to the flagship station telling you how impossible that is, you are scanning the sponsor's invoice statement that reads something to the effect, "Here is our purchase order for $1 million."

Your immediate supervisor says, "A MILLION DOLLARS?! Just DO IT!"

The administrative assistant now brings you a typical, daily stack of resumés, all of them begging to have some of your time because, "I really love sports. I played Little League when I was a kid." You throw them back at the assistant and tell her to file them.

The administrative assistant gives them to a college intern and tells her to file them with the others. At the end of the month, the administrative assistant tells the college intern to box up all the resumés in the file cabinet, and to ship them off to the warehouse for storage. They never got read.

This scenario repeats itself on a very regular basis, until finally, the director decides to read some of the resumés. She picks up a stack too big for her desk and starts looking at the front pages of a few of them, turning them rapidly. One catches her eye, and she pulls it from the stack. She decides to read every word on it at a later date. By the end of the stack, which was whipped through faster than the tornado that swept Dorothy from Kansas to Oz, the director has decided to read four resumés in depth.

Why Those Four?

Less than one percent of all job seekers in major-league sports know how to create a winning resumé. On top of that dreadful statistic is the depressing news that the average time a director spends reading a resumé is about 3½ seconds. How can you hope to beat the odds on that? Sometimes you can't. But believe it or not, there are some things in your resumé that can make it as if you were waving a red flag at the director, making him want to read more about you.

So, how do you go about producing the perfect resumé? You don't. There is no perfect resumé. While one director may be attracted to a resumé, a different director may be turned off by it. Stranger yet, a director's mood can also determine whether or not a resumé is good. On game day, it could be discarded because something important you had to say about yourself was missed. On a slow day, he or she would have loved to have called you up for an interview because the resumé happened to strike a different chord.

Wow, that seems completely beyond your control. Sometimes. However, you can increase the odds in your favor.

Caution! Don't keep sending a bad resumé. It's like shouting over and over again, "I'm a fool. I'm a fool!" You'll be killing off whatever chance you may have had. The best way to explain what is good and what is not, is to show actual samples (with names changed, of course).

> **BONUS HINT:**
> *Although the odds seem to weigh heavily against you, cheer up; the director who is too busy to read your resumé is also saying to himself, "I've got to find a way to get some help around here."* ***If your cover letter and resumé don't reflect that "helping" sentiment, you have no chance.*** *They simply don't care if you've always loved hockey.*

First of all, you need a cover letter. How important is this? It is essential. Do it. Regardless of how good you think your resumé is, regardless of how convinced you are that your resumé says it all and stands by itself, a cover letter is just easier to read.

Here are some general helpful tips:

♦ Keep it very, very short. Roadside billboards sell a lot of merchandise in this country, and they don't say much at all. They are designed for high-speed reading. The same concept applies in a cover letter asking for a job with a major-league sports franchise. State your case, and let it go. Your resumé can fill in the details. The job of your cover letter is to get the director to turn the page. Period.

> **BONUS HINT:**
>
> *Don't stop with a single submission of your resumé. Don't be a nuisance (please), but don't give up, either. Try again next month. Perhaps your resumé never got read. A phone call might not be a bad idea to see if your resumé was received. This usually forces the person at the other end to look for your resumé. Once it's out, it may end up on top of the pile. You may not get very far with a phone call, but at least it's an excuse to make one and get your name mentioned.*

♦ Use a lot of white space. It is much easier for the director to discard your resumé into the slush pile, than it is for him to speed-read a cluttered page with your life's history squeezed onto it. Remember the "billboard" example. Short, simple, make it stand out at high-speed driving. It's not meant to tell the whole story.

♦ Use oversized bullet points. This is like drawing a bull's-eye for the director to focus on. It works every time, even for directors who are in a hurry. Make that ESPECIALLY when in a hurry. But don't overdo it. Two or three will suffice.

♦ Say what you want in the first sentence. Don't make them guess, and don't make them keep reading to find out what position you are seeking. They won't do it. If you can't state what you want in the very first or second sentence, your next paragraph will never be read.

- Drop names if you can reasonably and truthfully do so. If you really do know the vice president, say so in the first sentence. If you met someone in the grocery store who knows the vice president, say so in the second sentence. If you saw the vice president buying groceries in the store, don't mention it at all. However, go kick yourself for not helping him to bag his groceries or at least holding the door open for him and saying hello.

- If you used to work for the Toronto Blue Jays, say so in the first sentence. If your brother used to work for the Toronto Blue Jays, say so in the second sentence. If you used to have Blue Jays season tickets, that's nice but so what?

- Don't send it by fax. It's black-and-white. It's dull. Maybe it came out on that stupid fax paper in a roll. Maybe it was on that unmanageable paper that curled up and got ink on everything. Maybe half of it got lost in the transfer. Maybe the director was out for a couple of days and the intern ditched it in the trash because it was left in the tray for too long. Don't fax. A day or two by postal mail won't kill you.

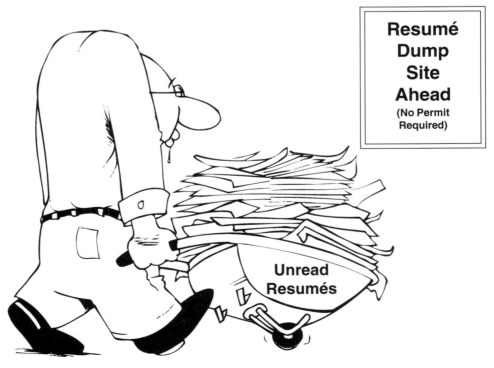

Resumé Dump Site Ahead
(No Permit Required)

Unread Resumés

♦ Use quality paper. DO NOT USE PERFORATED COM-PUTER PAPER. Use the same quality of paper that you imagine a professional sports franchise would use. Would they send out letters to major sponsors on the same paper you are using? If not, then why are you being so cheap and/or tacky when it comes to selling yourself? Another point, do not use a dot matrix printer if you can avoid it. Try to borrow a laser printer.

Actual Cover Letters:
The Good, The Bad and The Ugly

GOOD:

♦ "Here is something that I hope sticks in your mind." (He included a stick of chewing gum, pasted to the cover letter, wrapped in custom-designed paper with his name and address on it, as his "business card.")

(NOTE: Why is this "Good?" He was applying for a creative advertising position. Unless you are applying for the same position DO NOT ATTEMPT THIS AT HOME, BOYS AND GIRLS. It is otherwise TACKY.

BAD: (Opening Line)

♦ "I am graduating from college the first week in May and I need a job. What college graduate doesn't need a job?" (NOTE: Don't beg.)

UGLY: (Opening Line)

♦ "To Whom It May Concern:"

♦ "Dear Hiring Executive:"

♦ "Dear Human Resources:"

♦ "Dear Personnel Director:"

♦ "Dear Sirs:"

(NOTE: If you don't know the director's name, you are not ready to send your resumé and cover letter. Make a phone call first. Get the name and verify the spelling.)

GOOD: (Opening Line)

♦ "I am writing to express my interest in an internship in the public relations division of (team name)."

(NOTE: Perfect! Four Stars. And he got the internship, too.)

BAD:

♦ "I am writing to inquire about any job opportunities that may be available within your organization at this time."

(NOTE: Make up your mind and apply for a specific position. Don't say, "Your organization." Use the team name.)

UGLY:

♦ "I have followed the NBA since the '70s and have always wanted to become part of an organization."

♦ "My dad holds courtside season tickets and I have been a fan ever since the team came to town. I have a great deal of knowledge about basketball and am ready to learn even more. I am willing to work in any department. I am energetic and hardworking..."

♦ "I have always aspired to work in the world of professional sports. My enthusiasm and excitement for the National Basketball Association, with its continuing growth, along with your team's success, make me want to apply for whatever position you may have available."

♦ "It has been a lifelong goal of mine to work in professional athletics..."

GOOD:

♦ "I am seeking a summer internship in Marketing and Promotions with (team name). I will be available May 10 through Sept. 5."

BAD:

♦ "I have leadership skills, when necessary."

(NOTE: When necessary? You mean like on Mondays and Wednesdays you can lead, but the rest of the time, watch out?)

UGLY:

- "I had the good fortune of meeting (the team surgeon) when he (performed brain surgery) on my father."

(NOTE: Good fortune? This is name dropping at its worst!)

GOOD:

- "My name is (Jane Doe). I am a Junior at (State U). I am interested in doing an internship with your team during the summer of 1995." (NOTE: She was hired as an intern.)

BAD:

- "I am currently completing an internship in the Community Relations Department of the Detroit Pistons."

(NOTE: Why is this bad? Because it was buried in the middle of a cluttered cover page and got missed. This is the ULTIMATE type of experience you want to bring out. This sentence should be a neon sign in the middle of a large section of white space. Keep everything else out of it — STOP! Quit writing. You just got the page turned, and that is all you want a cover page to do. Name drop: DETROIT PISTONS.)

UGLY:

- "After graduating first in my class at (State University), I became a parnter (sic)..."

(NOTE: Typo in the first line of your cover letter. And it started so promising, too. Sorry, typos cannot go out to the public. They do, of course, but only from people who've already been hired.)

GOOD: (Almost)

- "I am seeking a full-time position with (team name)."

(NOTE: Forgot to mention what position. Otherwise he was short and to-the-point in saying what he wanted.)

BAD: (Opening Line)

- "Enthusiastic, creative, professional, motivated and dedicated; these traits characterize my personality and work ethic."

UGLY:

- "I am a self-starter who is looking to join a reputable organization that could benefit from an individual who is ready to give 110 percent."

(NOTE: Wasted space. Other examples of ramblings are listed below. Say what you have to say and get on with it.)

- "Studying literature at the University of (Name) has trained me to exercise my imagination, write clearly and analyze thoroughly — while also helping me to understand and empathize with other people. A year overseas helped me to adjust to other cultures ...."

- "I first became interested in working with elite athletes when, through classes, I discovered that this level of athlete is placed under tremendous amounts of stress. To further compound the problem, professional athletes are constantly on the road. Research has indicated, as well as experience, that traveling and the expectation of consistent performances by players is extremely difficult. However, if mentally prepared, the difficulty in this situation can be greatly reduced. I feel I would bring this same mental toughness to your organization ...."

GOOD:

- "I am writing to express my interest in your summer internship position. I spoke to you on the phone last week regarding this position..."

(NOTE: Great! She called, got a name, got a position, and wrote a quick reminder as her cover letter. The page got turned.)

BAD:

- "I have assembled press kits for Gatorade as well as edited their Sports Science Exchange Articles."

(NOTE: Bad? Why? Because Gatorade is a MAJOR sponsor for just about every professional sports franchise in America, and this sentence was buried in small print, in a clutter of paragraphs squeezed together on a lengthy cover letter. His cover letter should have read something like:

I am seeking full-time employment with the (Team name) in the area of sponsorship sales and promotions. I have experience in the following:

♦ GATORADE: Assembled press kits.

Sincerely,

UGLY:

♦ "I feel your organization can help my professional interests."

(NOTE: The director is searching for someone to help ***his own*** professional interests.)

GOOD: (Perfect Cover Letter in its Entirety)

"Dear Ms. (Name),

"I have enclosed an updated resumé for you in response to our telephone conversation. As I indicated, I am interested in an internship with your Marketing Department for this upcoming summer. I look forward to coming in for an interview. I appreciate your consideration.

Sincerely,

(Name)

NOTE: This is a great cover letter from a female college student looking for an internship. Study this carefully. It is four lines long. You could read it at a glance. She telephoned the team, got a specific name and actually talked to that person. She expressed interest in a specific department, and gave her availability dates. Whether or not she got the position is unimportant to a cover letter. This letter is successful in that it accomplishes its one and only goal — to get the cover page turned to the resumé.

The only possible way in which this cover letter could have been better would have been with one sentence leading in to a bullet list of experience. Each bullet point should be bold print or otherwise highlighted, listing related SPORTS activity or naming a previous internship with a PROFESSIONAL TEAM.

BAD:

♦ "I am writing to you because you know the value of a highly motivated, knowledgeable and enthusiastic person in your public relations department. I know, because I have been impressed with the marketability of your team, since you've had a winning season."

(NOTE: Would you want this person making statements like that in your press releases?)

UGLY:

♦ "Being from Cleveland, I have seen firsthand the excitement generated by the National Basketball Association. No other sport captures the imagination of fans of all ages, races and cultures, as does professional basketball. Basketball is rapidly approaching soccer as the world's most popular sport ...."

(NOTE: And on and on and on about basketball. What the heck does this guy want?)

GOOD:

♦ "I am seeking a position in advertising and promotions .... (experience listed in bullet points)

• NEW YORK YANKEES .... internship

• NEW YORK RANGERS .... internship

(NOTE: RED FLAG! DIRECTOR, GIVE THIS PERSON A CALL NOW! Never underestimate the value of having worked somewhere as a volunteer. Wouldn't YOU like to have something like this on your cover letter?)

Here is one more good cover letter, in its entirety, for you to study.

Dear Mr. (Name):

Please accept my resumé in consideration for future openings in your marketing/promotions departments. Please note that I have worked with your organization in the past. I voluntarily assisted (Staff member name) with the Opening

Night promotions. I worked very hard on this promotion and took great pride in its success. Thank you for your time.

Again, there are no rigid rules, but hopefully you can see the difference between a good cover letter and a bad one. If you've worked for a professional team, leave a lot of white space on your letter so the team name can jump out. The director will turn the page and glance at your resumé.

THANK-YOU

"Dear Mr. (Name):

Thank-you for the internship information. After reviewing my objectives for the internship and the opportunities available through (Team Name), I would like to apply for an internship in the summer of 1995 ... (One more short paragraph about her enclosed resumé, followed with the final close) I will telephone you on March 1 to discuss in more detail the goals of the position. Thank you for your time. I look forward to speaking with you soon."

Or:

"Dear Mr. (Name):

Thank-you for taking the time to speak with me this morning over the telephone. I realize that you have already extended an offer for the secretarial position in your department. If the status of the position changes, I would appreciate an opportunity to meet with you to discuss my qualifications in greater detail. Through my previous contacts with (Name drop another department director), I would enjoy being a part of (the team). Thank-you."

(NOTE: All this in one, short paragraph.)

Your Sports-Related Resumé

The purpose of your cover letter was to get the director to turn the page to your resumé. The purpose of your resumé is to get a personal interview. As with the cover letter, there are no rigid rules on what a resumé should contain. But there are certain portions of a resumé that should stand out. You want to have enough detail in your resumé to get that interview, but not enough to give your whole sales pitch. You'll do that in person.

For now, make sure that the best features of your resumé are prominently displayed, with white space for a border, bold lettering or underlining, or bullet points. The resumé should have more content than your "billboard theory" on the cover letter, but not enough to force you to use small type fonts to squeeze all the information onto a page. Use two pages if necessary. Paper clip them together. Never staple.

> **BONUS HINT:**
> *Directors scan very quickly for highlighted Key Words, especially names of other pro franchises for whom you've worked. If you've never worked for a pro franchise, do everything possible to volunteer for one. Next, minor leagues; next, college. Find something you can highlight that reflects SPORTS.*

The second page (or the third page) should be used to list your references. Do not say you'll give references upon request. They want them now, if they want you now.

Some common segments that make up the whole resumé are:

√ Awards/Achievements
√ College Activities
√ Computer Skills
√ Education
√ Name/Address/Phone
√ Objective
√ Personal
√ References
√ Related Experience
√ Salary Requirements
√ Special Interests/Hobbies
√ Summary
√ Work Experience

Do not use every portion above to construct your resumé. Use only those parts that are pertinent, and put first those that highlight your best attributes.

NAME/ADDRESS/PHONE

Put this at the top. Do not assume that your cover letter has stayed intact with your resumé. Assume it got lost in the stack, and that you need to include your name, address and phone number on every page.

OBJECTIVE

This goes next.

ITS ONLY PURPOSE IS TO STATE IN ONE SENTENCE WHAT YOU WANT.

Do not include a vague paragraph at the top labeled OBJECTIVE, and then proceed to ramble about working habits and chances for advancement and getting to use your skills and remunerations that match your abilities.

GOOD:

- ◆ "Full-time employment in sponsorship sales with the (Team Name)."
- ◆ "To obtain a media relations position with the (Team Name).
- ◆ "To work in sports television production with (Team Name)."
- ◆ "Desire an accounting position."

(NOTE: Don't forget to mention the team's name. The resumé shouldn't look like you photocopied them en masse.)

OK FOR NOW:

- ◆ "A sports marketing/sales position that will enable me to put into practice my managerial and marketing skills." NOTE: Leave out the rambling part after "sales position."

- ◆ "Seeking an internship in a management position with a sports related corporation." NOTE: She said she wanted an internship, fine. But, do NOT give the appearance of mass producing this resumé. Say you are seeking a specific position, with their team. Which director gets this resumé? If this gets mailed to a specific director, it's OK.

- ◆ "To enter the exciting world of the NBA with an entry-level position in the field of public relations, marketing or sales." NOTE: Leave out the part about the exciting world of the NBA. Also, too many positions. Which director gets this? If the envelope was addressed to a specific director, though, then this is perfectly OK.

WRONG:

♦ "To obtain a challenging position with the opportunity to contribute to the efficient operation of the company, utilizing creativity and complementing the ideas of others, and to also earn advancement through on-the-job performance."

NOTE: Wasted space that says nothing. Say what you want in one line and get on with it.

Many resumés don't say anything at all about an objective, nor do they say anywhere on the resumé what they want. At the top, don't forget to say what you want in one line.

♦ "To obtain a position which will allow me to use my education, experience, and strong work ethic to benefit my employer, as well as myself."

♦ "An internship in a professional sports organization where I can use my problem-solving skills and gain valuable experience in the world of sports, leading to career opportunities with potential for advancement."

> ## BONUS HINT:
> *"Related Experience" is more important than courses you took in school. Unless your resumé reflects experience in sports, you won't get a job, or even an internship. Volunteer in your school or community. When you get several experiences, list the most important first and drop the least important. When you can include a pro franchise, you are ready to seek permanent employment in the big leagues.*

EMPLOYMENT HISTORY

Unless it is filled with sports-related positions, do not label a section as this. Instead, call it "RELATED EXPERIENCES." Then proceed to list your sports background, leaving out non-related employment histories.

RELATED EXPERIENCES

If your work history (or volunteer portfolio) does not include at least two sports-related descriptions, you are not yet ready to apply for employment with a major-league sports franchise. You must have experience. Find out what sporting events are coming to town, amateur or professional, and volunteer your services in some capacity. Continue to do so until you have several items to place on your resumé under the heading called "RELATED EXPERIENCES."

They don't care if you work at WalMart or McDonald's or Acme Insurance. They want to see something, such as these actual resumé segments:

♦ Cleveland Lumberjacks (International Hockey League):

♦ Intern with Vice President of Sales, 1994, Summer. Solicited and sold season tickets to corporations and private persons. Assisted public relations department with promotional campaigns.

♦ Miami University Athletic Department: Intern with Assistant Athletic Director, 1993-94. Assisted with planning of promotional activities. Operated souvenir stand and promotional tables.

The Related Experiences section depends upon which department you are considering. If you want sports merchandising then mention your job with the local athletic store packing sweat pants and T-shirts.

If you want broadcast production, mention the college radio and television stations you interned with. Volunteer to be a runner for the crews during the football and basketball broadcasts.

You must "build" a sports-related resumé. Volunteer. Volunteer. Volunteer. Besides, it's usually fun to get involved. It's entertainment.

EDUCATIONAL BACKGROUND

If this is a weak point, such as old information, or no college, keep it minute, or even list it under a different heading. If it is a strong point, such as having graduated in the top five percent at Harvard University in Marketing Management, highlight it.

CAUTION: Too many applicants list college sporting experiences under this heading. If you WORKED or VOLUNTEERED in a sports-related capacity at your school, list it under RELATED EXPERIENCES, not under educational background.

AWARDS/ACHIEVEMENTS

Usually this is not included unless you have something like the following real resumés:

♦ "Was selected to represent Foot Locker at its team store in Charlotte, N.C., at the 1994 NCAA Championship."

NOTE: And even this is wrong — it should have been put into the RELATED EXPERIENCES section, although it is highlighted and still is prominent on the page:

♦ "Who's Who in America, President's Honor Roll, Valedictorian, National Honor Society."

COLLEGE ACTIVITIES

A major mistake is using this section to describe RELATED EXPERIENCES. College activities are not important on a sports resumé unless they depict sports activities. In such cases, they should go in RELATED EXPERIENCES.

COMPUTER SKILLS

Wow, is this ever getting vital. If you can't use a computer, you are going to be a major headache to the department, and all other departments who get delayed while you mess around trying to get out the information. This should go last, unless you are applying for a technical position. Simply mention which software programs you know. You don't have to be good, just adequate. Very few people in the franchise will be "good" with a computer ... just comfortable using one. Don't get scared over it, but be prepared.

PERSONAL

If you feel there is something important, then say it. Otherwise, it is not necessary to know if you are married, in good health and 30 years old. Save it for the personal interview.

REFERENCES

NEVER say you will give references later. Include them now, with no exceptions. Put them on a separate page and paper clip them to your resumé. Use sports-related references whenever possible. If you don't know anyone in sports, you are not ready to submit a resumé.

SALARY REQUIREMENTS

Save it for later. You have no idea as to a team's budget. Giving a wrong salary range may either kill your chances at a job or cheat you out of a better salary. Don't chance it.

SPECIAL INTERESTS/HOBBIES

Who cares? If you play golf on weekends with the team's biggest sponsor, then say so.

SUMMARY

This section of a resumé is becoming more popular. It is usually placed at the top instead of using an OBJECTIVE. However, if you go this route, put your objective in the very first line, stating exactly what you want. Then state your summary of qualifications, if you must. CAUTION: Summarizing your qualifications, more often than not, leads to rambling. However, if it gives you the opportunity to throw in another "Name Dropping," then do it. Otherwise, play it safe with a one-line OBJECTIVE.

You are your own best salesperson. There are no hard, fast rules to follow on a resumé, but if you venture too far off from what has been mentioned in this chapter, you are more apt to make a fool out of yourself rather than land a job. Use whatever resumé segments you feel best highlight your qualifications for SPORTS. Leave out every unnecessary word.

Once again, use a type and style of paper that you would expect to receive from this franchise if it was to write to you. Anything less tells them that you are not of the same quality. Anything more, and you've gone overboard.

Do not use strange or fancy type fonts. Do not use "script" or "Old English" because they are difficult to read.

Make your resumé no more than two pages, excluding the reference sheet, which would be a third page. Any longer and the director won't read it, regardless of your qualifications. The warehouse is full of resumés from qualified people who made them too difficult for the director. Keep them short and simple.

5

Personal

Interview

Do's and Don'ts

OK, so the resumé is sent, the contacts contacted, and all your networking has paid off into snagging an interview.

Now what?

Don't panic, but you need to be clear on what type of interview it is. Is the interviewer just being nice and giving you an "informational interview" because he owes one of your contacts a favor, or is there a real job opening that the franchise will definitely fill?

If it's the former, go with notebook in hand and a list of questions. But in between fact-finding, make a sales pitch on your behalf so if there is an opening some day, the interviewer might remember your wit and wisdom.

If it's the latter, go to the interview confident that you are the right person for the position. Depending on the level of the position, most sports teams won't interview more than three people for any job, so your chances of success are good. Follow these Do's and Don'ts and your chances can rise from good to excellent.

Setting the Time

You get the call asking you to come in for an interview.

DO: Set the date and time for as soon as possible.

DON'T: Delay.

While you are procrastinating about when you'll have time to get that new outfit or see your hairdresser, someone else will have had an opportunity to impress the interviewer. In sports, there's what is known as a "window of opportunity," a short span of time in which you have an opportunity to take advantage of a career situation before the door slams shut. The point is, there is always somebody ready to take your spot if you hesitate.

Most companies like to fill openings (or at least make the decisions on who should fill those openings) as soon as possible. Handle one situation and move onto the next. Drop what you are doing and make an appointment for the next day.

Doing Research

Hopefully, before sending out a resumé you at least know something about the franchise.

DO: Find out everything you can about the club in as short a time as possible.

DON'T: Wing it.

Use your contacts to see if you can dig up a team media guide, program or yearbook. Find a biography, if possible, on the interviewer. See if you have common ground — the same alma mater, a fondness for golf or whatever might make for interesting small talk at the beginning of the interview. Check the newspapers from the last few days to see if the team has made any transactions on or off

the field. You can break the ice by asking if the acquisition of Peter Hardthrower will change the club's pitching rotation. See if you can uncover financial information about the team in a local library.

If the team is constantly in the red, stress in the interview how you are one to generate revenues and keep a close eye on the bottom line. If you have an inside source, find out why the job opening exists. Was the previous employee fired, promoted? Or did he leave for personal reasons? Is it a newly created position? If you can, even find out exactly the type of person being sought. Knowledge is power and the more knowledge you have of the franchise going in, the better impression you will make.

Making a Good Impression

It's a cliche, but it's true: You only get one chance to make a first impression.

DO: Make a good impression.

DON'T: Take any chances.

Dress the part. You are seeking a front office job with a professional sports team. Proper attire for an interview for men and women is a conservative business suit, a solid white or lightly colored shirt, a conservative tie, plain socks or hose, and freshly polished shoes. Be well groomed in all other areas, too (hair, nails, etc.). Even if you are going for a creative or fun job with a team, dress conservatively at the interview. If you are going for a job as creative director at MTV, then be artsy and funky. But since you want to work in sports, start out conservative and lighten up as is appropriate once you land the job.

Be on time. There is never a good enough excuse for being late to an interview. Plan on arriving early and leave time to find a parking lot and the proper office. Make a last-second check in a mirror before entering the office.

Add to the good visual impression with a strong handshake during introductions and appropriate casual conversation before the interview begins. If there is any doubt about whether you should address the interviewer by his first or last name, choose the safe way out. He probably won't care if you use his first name, but some people are still picky about such a thing. Say, "Hello, Mr. Doe." He'll tell you to call him, "John."

When entering the interviewer's office, check the wall for pictures or plaques which might be good conversation pieces. See if a family photo on the desk reveals a young son in a soccer uniform. Anything that can start small talk will not only make you more comfortable, but make the interviewer more comfortable, too. Most interviewers don't perform job interviews every day, and they can be just as uncomfortable in the situation as you are. Break the ice. Be pleasant and sincere. Don't be sharp-tongued or obnoxious. Make eye contact and be aware of your posture and body language.

Answering the Questions

Let the questioning begin.

DO: Give brief, serious answers to all queries.

DON'T: Go into such detail that the interviewer doesn't have a chance to ask the next question.

In answering the questions about your skills, give personal anecdotes showing how you have the experience to do the job. If you describe how you've done it in the past, it will paint a mental image with the interviewer of you doing the job. If you just tell the interviewer that you feel confident you can do the job, the interviewer may have doubts. So, create as many positive mental pictures as you can.

> ### BONUS HINT:
> *The purpose of most job interviews is, first, to find out if you are capable of handling the position, and second, if you have the ability to communicate and get along with people.*

Humorous asides can help break the ice, but don't perform a comedy routine. Saying the wrong thing is even worse than wearing a bad suit. Give meaning to your words, and don't just talk for the sake of making conversation. To show that you have an ability to communicate, ask some questions of your own. Don't get into benefits (wait until an offer is made), but ask about possible assignments or projects that you might encounter.

If for some reason you have gotten an interview without having first presented your resumé for review (he told you over the phone to come on in), then don't hand him your resumé the very first thing. You want him to look at your face, and remember you. If you give him your resumé the very first thing, it is only natural for him to keep perusing it as you talk. Save it for last — he can read it when you are gone, unless there are specific points you want to cover.

If it is pertinent, show the interviewer your job samples. If there is important information about you that you want the interviewer to know, find a way of getting to it. Don't ignore a question to get to your information, but get the conversation around to what you feel is important. If possible, practice a Q-and-A with someone who has gone through an interview or two. Throughout the whole ordeal, try to remain relaxed. You'll be better with your responses and create a good impression.

Following Up

You aren't done, yet.

DO: Thank the interviewer for his or her time.

DON'T: Hound the interviewer and force him or her to make a decision on the spot.

> ### *BONUS HINT:*
>
> *Know the appropriate jargon. Speak the language. If the interviewer uses common, ordinary abbreviations for the business, and you don't understand, he'll know you don't have any experience. Make this part of your research, if necessary.*

It probably won't hurt you to ask in a sheepish way, "How'd I do?" as you are walking to the door. Who knows, the interviewer might commit to something before they complete all their other interviews. Find out when a decision will be made. Send a thank you note to the interviewer. Keep it simple and restate your desire to work for that team. Don't fill the note with things you wished you had said in the interview. Have your contacts call the interviewer to endorse you and offer follow-up information. Then, depending on the situation, you might want to telephone the interviewer a few days later to ask if a decision has been made.

Even if the decision isn't in your favor, don't fret. Remember, the person they offer the job to might not accept it. You might be the runner-up ready to fill in. Or, there may be another job opening a short time later and a good impression might carry over to that situation. But even if there is no job, consider it good training. You've gone through an interview, which will make you even more prepared for the next one. And hopefully, by asking a few questions you've learned a bit more about the industry you want to enter.

6

Where Do You Go From Here?

Hopefully by now, you've absorbed enough information from this book to believe that you really can attain that front office dream job with a professional sports franchise. And, yes, for many it really is a dream come true to get a career in one of the world's most exciting industries, sports.

Although salaries and benefits vary greatly, especially in the lesser skilled positions, it is no secret that a sports franchise can pay an extraordinary amount of money to a valuable employee, especially in upper management where perks and benefits can nearly match the income itself.

Professional, major-league teams won't send you on a trip by car or put you up in a cheap motel. You'll fly a major airline, sometimes first class or charter, and stay in highly rated hotels with ample per diem in your pocket to eat and shop at your desire.

But even more than the value of the physical items you may receive in exchange for your skills, is the intangible treasure of enjoyment. Working a labor of love. How valuable is that?

Most of your family and friends will begrudgingly crawl out of bed in the morning, dreading to go to work. They live for the weekends, when they can sleep in. They go to work, doing something they don't really enjoy. They anticipate breaks, and drag themselves back to work after lunch. They rush to their cars at five o'clock and speed home, where they grab a quick burger, read the paper, watch the news, a program or two on television, then hit the sack until it's time to wake up and do it again.

They break the monotony by taking a two-week vacation once a year, or by watching the Big Game on television, wishing they were at the arena in person.

You, on the other hand, jump out of bed before the alarm clock has a chance to ring. In fact, you may never even set the alarm. If your friends were going to Disney World early in the morning, they'd be jumping out of bed, too. Maybe you're not going to Disney World (unless you win the championship), but going to work can be just as much fun at times. Imagine the thrill of getting a ticket to the World Series, the Super Bowl, the Stanley Cup playoffs or the NBA Finals. Now imagine that you are down on the field or court, conversing with the players beforehand. How cool is that? Your family and friends will grant you celebrity status for mingling with the players they see from a distance.

Therein lies the problem. Who wouldn't want to do that?

Unfortunately, competition for such a career is fierce. Just as there are no long lines in a bad restaurant, there is no flood of applicants for a bad job. With a career in the Big Show as the prize, you'll discover that multitudes are trying to get in the same front door as you. Therefore, you need to do everything in your power to gain the competitive advantage and improve the odds in your favor.

Everything about you must shout to the director that you are front office material from Day 1. Unlike the team coach, who has time to develop young rookies by sitting them on the bench for a couple of years, the front office director has no such luxury. Of course you are not expected to know the daily routines of a specific franchise on your first day of employment, but you should be at home, able to run the position without supervision within a relatively short time span.

A career in sports is great, but there are some disadvantages to be aware of, the greatest being the pressure to get your job done on time. The game is going to start according to the scheduled time, whether or not you are ready. Have you ever been outside the arena gate, waiting impatiently for the ushers and ticket takers to open up? Have you ever watched a game on television when the broadcast station loses the picture? Or the sound? Have you ever seen a station break where, instead of a commercial, you see the cue card that says something like, "Slot 2A here."

Have you ever gone to your seat, only to find that someone else was already sitting there, and they had the same ticket as you? Have you ever seen the scoreboard go out during a game? Or the clock? Have you ever seen the dance squad get out of sync? Have you ever noticed when the team mascot and his crew didn't run their routine as smoothly as planned? Maybe you've been cut off during the transfer of a call to the front office. Maybe they can't find your ticket in Will Call.

There are any number of things that can go wrong when working in the entertainment field. And you know what? The fans really don't care as to why or why not such-and-such didn't go right — it just didn't, that's all. Do it right. Get it done on time. The Show is going on without you. You cannot say, "Sorry folks, there are no programs available for tonight's game because my computer crashed."

Can you understand, now, why directors may not always have time to sit and read cover letters and resumés? It's not that they don't care if you've always loved sports, and that your dad is a season ticket holder, or that you really need a job so you can get married. The director simply has priorities, and there is never enough time.

> **BONUS HINT:**
>
> *When you talk to the director, he is thinking about one of two scenarios:*
>
> *1. "I got some good help today. I won't have to work so late every night," or:*
>
> *2. "Honey, I'll have to work late again, tomorrow. This new guy just can't get the job done."*
>
> *Which of the above would you be to that director? He doesn't care about anything else.*

The would-be successful applicant is the one who will give the impression of being able to alleviate some of the stress from the director, and to make sure everything gets done as planned without excuse. He cannot have an intern tell him, "I couldn't get to the airport and pick up the half-time entertainer because the company van didn't start." The successful candidate is the one who is able to let the director go home on time and tell his wife, "I got some good help today. I won't have to work so late every night."

Repeat: "I got some good help today. I won't have to work so late every night." That is what the director wants to know. That is why he accepts or rejects you. You are a good, reliable helper. You can take over some of his everyday duties to free him up. He doesn't want someone he has to train for a lengthy period. He doesn't want to go home late and say, "Honey, I'll have to work late again, tomorrow. This new guy just can't get the job done."

Very few professional sports franchises make you punch a clock. Very few keep track of when you take a break, when you go to lunch, or even when you go home. Seldom does a supervisor stand over an employee to supervise. You are expected to be a professional and to get the job done, on time, in good fashion, without supervision. And if you were to ask most people on the street, they would tell you that a situation like that should be considered a benefit, not a drawback. You are your own person. Just do it.

Other than that, there really are not too many drawbacks to a career in sports once you get your foot in the door and get established. You'll have your rough moments getting started due to the competition talked about throughout this book. Volunteer work for little or no pay can cause some financial hardships, as you must be aware. How will you pay the bills working for minimum wage? Everyone in sports has dealt with this problem, so don't be ashamed. It goes with the territory.

Stick with it and those problems vanish. You will be so busy doing your job to the best of your ability that all of a sudden you'll wonder where all that extra money came from at the end of the month, assuming of course, that you are entering into a sports career with the idea of advancing through the ranks.

The amazing thing is how much opportunity there is for advancement if you are willing to relocate, and if you are willing to work for different teams in various sports. If you stick with the same thing your whole life, you are limiting yourself. Look again at the advice you got from the insiders. They went from selling tickets to football games in Cleveland to directing game operations for hockey in California. Be flexible at all levels of employment in professional sports, from general manager on down to where you are now, an outsider trying desperately to get a foot in the door.

You can do it. You'll be amazed at the number of applicants you will have gotten the upper hand on simply because of studying this book and applying the principles here. During the time it took you to read this book, there have been thousands of aspiring sports-career enthusiasts who've dropped resumés into the mailbox, telling Whom It May Concern how much they love baseball, and they'd like a job in the Department of Anything because they are enthusiastic, hard-working and dedicated.

You, on the other hand, can now smile at such a faux pas.

So, what now? What should you do?

For starters, you now know that only a few words of each resumé are ever read. Do you remember which words are like flashing neon lights, depending upon the position? They are those words that tell the director, "Hey, I've already done this many, many times with reputable franchises. Matter of fact, our team beat yours in the playoffs." The director knows you can do the job, because he deals with that team on a regular basis. He knows what you've been through.

Does your portfolio reflect that kind of experience? Probably not. *But now you know where to start.*

- Build your resumé.
- Fill it with flashing neon signs.
- Be able to name drop professional franchises for whom you've worked.

But that doesn't make sense, you say? If you could fill your resumé with an employment history filled with big-league names, then you wouldn't be reading this book.

That, dear friend, is the one thing that you CAN control, the one problem you CAN overcome. How? It's that old vicious circle: How can you get experience if nobody will hire you?

Start as high in the career ladder as you can, yet keep going as low as you have to, in order to get that first assignment, be it a paid job with a Rookie League team, or as a volunteer position with the local YMCA traveling basketball team. Some candidates are lucky enough (although they put themselves into a position of being able to get lucky) to gain an unpaid internship with a major-league franchise their very first attempt. (And even then, "Uncle Charley" probably told them how silly they were to be working for "Nothin'.")

If you are wondering why this book keeps emphasizing the need to volunteer, to work for nothing if necessary (of course, don't quit looking for "paid" work), it is because, quite frankly, most people reading this book will either not believe the value of volunteering, or else they won't submit to starting in so low of a position, due probably to peer pressure or wrong expectations based upon bad advice from people who mean well.

That college course you are taking in sports management is great, but why aren't you working with the Homecoming Committee? It's nice that you are studying sports marketing, but why aren't you ushering the basketball games? It's too bad for all those people who read this paragraph and don't take it literally. The truth is, just taking that course

> ### BONUS HINT:
> *A sports course without sports experience is generally useless.*

won't do you a bit of good, without experience, somewhere, doing anything, for a sporting event.

Not long ago, professional sports franchises from every major sport assembled in Indianapolis, Ind., for what was billed as, "The Ultimate Sports Career Workshop." As insider after insider stressed the value of internships and volunteer work, the participants sighed, then laughed, at the thought of working for nothing. Then an Executive Director for one of the United States Olympic teams asked if anyone would be willing to volunteer to help her work at the World Championships!

Egads! Nobody volunteered. Can you believe it? What would you have done? Would you have raised your hand in jubilation? Would you have run home and told your family and friends, "I'm working at the World Championships for the United States Olympic team!"

What will you do, when your peers say, "You mean you're working for nuthin'?"

STOP RIGHT HERE! What will you tell the director during your personal interview, when he says, "Wow. You worked the World Championships for Team USA?" Did you catch the meaning of this paragraph?

DURING YOUR PERSONAL INTERVIEW!

That, my friend, is how you get in the front door. You have total control over much of your luck in landing a dream job in sports. You determine how badly you really want to be down on that basketball court with those superstars, shooting a few hoops with them in warmups. You start at the highest level you can, and be willing to go as low as necessary. You do this again, and again, and again.

Suddenly, your resumé reads:

- ◆ McClellan Racing Team — sponsorship sales, part-time
- ◆ Team USA — World Championships
- ◆ Hoboken Huskies — minor-league bocce ball
- ◆ YMCA — laundered uniforms

Would you rather have your resumé read about your sports course in college, and how you are presently working as a manager with a car rental firm, and how you managed a sales crew for an insurance company, and were the assistant in charge of such-and-such with so-and-so company?

IT DOES NOT COUNT.

Volunteer. Intern. Volunteer. Intern. Volunteer. Intern. That non-paying sporting event is going to be your money in the bank some-day.

There once was a lowly janitor named George Shinn. Now, there is Mr. George Shinn, owner of the Charlotte Hornets. Now when someone speaks to him about a "Sweep," it takes on a whole new meaning.

Now, it's YOUR turn. How much do you want that sports career? There are so many opportunities it is impossible to name them all. The whole world is bonkers about sports. Since you began reading this book, someone, somewhere has started a new league, or a new team, or maybe even a new sport. Not only is there an ESPN to broadcast sports, there is now an ESPN2!

Crazy. The whole world is crazy when it comes to sports. Sporting events are all around you. How can you NOT have several of them on your resumé. The only answer, it would appear to a direc-tor, is that you do not really want a sports career, you just want a ticket to the game. Otherwise, you'd be asking the Chamber of Com-merce, or a similar council in your local town, about sporting events coming to your area. Then, you'd be contacting that organizing body about helping them to paint the lines on the field. For *NUTHIN'*. You must be crazy to do that, your friends will say.

Yes, because you, too, are crazy about sports. And just as sure as the sun will rise in the morning, those same friends will be asking you, "Can you get me a ticket?" And, "Can you get me an autograph of Johnny Touchdown?"

Then, after being envious of your career, they too will write the Miami Dolphins and tell them how much they love the National Football League, and the Dolphins have been their favorite team for years, and they even used to watch way back when "Flipper" was the team mascot, and they'll take a towel boy job in the anything department, if they could get an interview with the director of hiring. But, they ain't gonna work for nuthin.'

Do-It-Yourself Career

Want to work in sports and work for yourself at the same time? Don't forget about paving your own career path. A lady who used to sell tickets for an NBA team recently created the Official NBA Trivia Game, licensed by the league and sold worldwide. She had her eye set on making her own promotions and setting her own destiny. She works with sports personnel on a regular basis.

Perhaps you should explore a similar path if you have management abilities and a willingness to hold your own event or start your own business.

Did you know, for example, that you can have an Olympic Governing Body actually sanction a rowing event, or a diving event, or whatever area you are interested in, once you meet the criteria? Make it a yearly event that could be quite profitable to you.

Another entrepreneur is a former basketball player who has a business matching up high school athletes with Division II colleges. Imagine all the games he gets to watch.

If you simply want a job about sports, but not necessarily working with sports personnel, there are numerous examples of successful trading card companies, fantasy sports leagues and newsletters. It satisfies their cravings for sports, and it beats going to work for a living.

One man in Atlanta has a business hiring sports stars, through their agents, for autograph sessions in which fans get to pay a fee and get a famous player's autograph. Talk about a dream job. When someone asks if he can get such-and-such autograph, he can just about always say yes ... for a 10-spot, of course. These sessions are becoming more and more common. Maybe you should entertain putting together your own show.

Another good starting point is finding an auto racing team and helping it find sponsors. Racing is very expensive, and even the best teams need sponsorship money. A person with revenue-generating abilities will find a job just about anywhere.

It's time for you to determine your own area of interest. Nobody can do that for you. Set your goals and make a plan. You can do it.

Good luck.

7

Sometimes, It's "WHO YOU KNOW"

"Oh, no. Say it ain't so."

You mean after this whole book, it might get down to your competition walking into the director's office and saying, "Hello, Uncle Bob."

Sadly, yes. That's life. It happens not only in sports, but everywhere. Job openings are seldom advertised, and if they are, it's only after offering the job to everyone else in the company. However, that means there will still be an opening for the person's job who took the promotion. Sometimes that job is filled by Uncle Bob's nephew.

The good news is ... it doesn't happen as often as you might think. Uncle Bob's nephew might not be able to do the job, and that still counts for more than anything else. Uncle Bob does not want to get fired when the computers crash on game day because of his inept nephew.

In sports, when the director asks other staff members, "Who Do You Know," he really means "Who Do You Know Who Can Do This Job Well?"

Therefore, you must make sure you know as many staff members as possible.

Repeat: You must make sure you know as many staff members as possible.

Once more: You must make sure you know as many staff members as possible.

Please take note that out of all the valuable advice you've discovered from this book, the above statement is the only one repeated three times.

One way to know staff members is to live near one, and to go visit him at work. Take the front office "tour." Meet everyone in the office. By far the best way to meet staff members is to do volunteer work at a sporting event. Bear in mind that the person for whom you are painting the lines on that field may someday be the director of such-and-such. In fact, this happens every day.

The more you volunteer, the better your chances are that someone you worked for will now be in a position to hire you. This is your surest bet for a career in sports.

This pattern of knowing staff members, who know staff members, who can get you a volunteer position with another staff member, is called "Networking."

Networking is vital in sports careers. You will spend your whole career networking. The Group Sales Manager of the Hornets will become the Director of Ticket Sales for the Pittsburgh Steelers, who will become the Vice President of Marketing for the Los Angeles Lakers. And he really appreciates the good work you did for him when you painted those lines.

> ### ULTIMATE BONUS HINT:
> *If you want a career in sports, go paint the foul lines on the baseball diamond of the Knucksville Knights — for nuthin'. It's crazy, but it works. Someday you may be with the New York Yankees.*

This is reality. This is the "Who You Know," more often than not. It's not Uncle Bob's nephew as much as it is, "He's the guy who helped with Opening Night when I worked for the Knucksville Knights."

A Networker's Dream Team of Names and Numbers

Remember: Call first. The person who is supposed to be the ticket manager for the Blue Jays may now be with the Cardinals.

NATIONAL BASKETBALL ASSOCIATION

645 Fifth Ave.

New York, NY 10022

(212) 407-8000

ATLANTA HAWKS

One CNN Center
Suite 405, South Tower
Atlanta, GA 30303
(404) 827-3800

President	Stan Kasten
Exec. VP	Lee Douglas
VP/GM	Pete Babcock
Dir./Media Relations	Arthur Triche
Dir./Marketing	Frank Timmerman
Dir./Community Affairs	Mel Pender
Controller/Business Mgr.	Cynthia Wilsky
Dir./Sales	Dan Taylor
Dir./Broadcast-Corp. Sales	Bill Schneider

BOSTON CELTICS

151 Merrimac St.
Boston, MA 02114
(617) 523-6050

President	Red Auerbach
Exec. VP/GM	Jan Volk
VP/Finance	Joseph G. DiLorenzo
VP/Planning-Special Events	Stuart Layne
VP/Marketing-Commun.	Tod Rosensweig
VP/Sales	Stephen Riley
VP	Tom McGrath
Dir./Sales	Duane Johnson
Dir./Public Relations	Jeff Twiss
Dir./Publications and Info.	David Zuccaro
Dir./Marketing	Mark Lev
Dir./Promos-Special Events	Kevin Martinez

CHARLOTTE HORNETS

100 Hive Drive
Charlotte, NC 28217
(704) 357-0252

President	Spencer Stolpen
VP/Business Operations	Sam Russo
VP/Marketing	Tom Ward
VP/Corp. Development	Roger Schweickert
VP/Finance	Wayne DeBlander
Dir./Media Relations	Harold Kaufman
Dir./Broadcast Operations	Steve Martin
Dir./Public Relations	Marilynn Bowler
Dir./Community Relations	Suzanne Conley
Dir./Publications	Bo Hussey
Dir./Ticket Operations	Clayton Smith
Controller	Shoon Ledyard

CHICAGO BULLS

1901 W. Madison St.
Chicago, IL 60612
(312) 455-4000

VP/Basketball Operations	Jerry Krause
VP/Financial & Legal	Irwin Mandel
VP/Marketing-Broadcasting	Steve Schanwald
Controller	Stu Bookman
Dir./Ticket Sales	Keith Brown
Dir./Media Services	Tim Hallam
Dir./Community Ser.	Sara Kalstone Salzman
Dir./Community Relations	Bob Love
Dir./Ticket-Stadium Operations	Joe O'Neil

CLEVELAND CAVALIERS

1 Center Court
Cleveland, OH 44115
(216) 420-2000

CEO/Business Division .... John Graham
President-COO/Team Div. .... Wayne Embry
President-COO/Business Div. .... Tom Chestnut
Sr. VP/Sales and Marketing .... Jim Kahler
VP/Broadcasting ....Joe Tait
VP/Finance .... Gene Weber
Dir./Public Relations .... Bob Price
Dir./Corp. Communications .... Gayle Bibby-Creme
Dir./Marketing .... John Cimperman
Sr. Dir./Corp. and Suite Sales .... Dave Auker
Sr. Dir./Ticket Sales .... Andy Malitz
Dir./Community Relations .... Lynn Charles
Dir./Broadcast Services .... David Dombrowski
Dir./Community and Business
 Development .... Austin Carr

DALLAS MAVERICKS

Reunion Arena, 777 Sports St.
Dallas, TX 75207
(214) 748-1808

Owner & President .... Donald Carter
COO/GM ....Norm Sonju
VP/Counsel .... Doug Adkins
Dir./Finance .... Jim Livingston
Dir./Media Services .... Kevin Sullivan
Dir./Operations .... Steve Letson
Dir./Marketing .... Mike Sheehan
Controller .... Tom Kelly

DENVER NUGGETS

McNichols Sports Arena
1635 Clay St.
Denver, CO 80204
(303) 893-6700

Sr. Exec. VP/GM .... Bernie Bickerstaff
Exec. VP .... Shawn Hunter
VP/Business Operations .... Gary Hunter
VP/CFO .... Mark Waggoner
VP/Broadcasting .... Lou Personett
Dir./Marketing .... Michael Blake
Creative Dir. .... Daniel Price
Dir./Ticket Operations .... Kirk Dyer
Dir./Administration .... Cheryl Miller
Dir./Retail Operations .... Scott Franklin
Dir./Corporate Sales/Services .... Chris Whitney
Dir./Special Events .... Deb Dowling
Dir./Community Relations ...... Kathleen MacDonald
Dir./Ticket Sales-Game Operations .... Joe Levy
Media Relations Dir. .... Tommy Sheppard

DETROIT PISTONS

The Palace of Auburn Hills
Two Championship Drive
Auburn Hills, MI 48326
(810) 377-0100

President .... Tom Wilson
Exec. VP ....Dan Hauser
Exec. VP .... John Ciszewski
Exec. VP .... Ron Campbell
VP/Public Relations .... Matt Dobek
VP/Marketing and Broadcasting .... Harry Hutt
VP/Advertising Sales .... Lou Korpas
VP/Sales ....Andy Appleby
VP/Multimedia Communications .... Pete Skorich
Dir./Media Relations .... Bill Wickett

GOLDEN STATE WARRIORS

Oakland Coliseum Arena
7000 Coliseum Way
Oakland, CA 94621
(510) 638-6300

President/CEO .... Andy Dolich
GM ....Dave Twardzik
VP/Broadcasting .... David McGahey
Dir./Marketing .... Andy Dallin
Dir./Media Relations .... Julie Marvel
Dir./Events & Game Operations .... Jim Rogers
Dirs./Community Relations .... Fran Miller, Nate
 Thurmond
TV Producer/Director .... Dan Becker
Ticket Mgr. .... Tim Barrett
Merchandise Mgr. .... Jim Sweeney
Dir./Sponsor Sales .... Todd Santino
Art Dir. .... Larry Hausen

HOUSTON ROCKETS

The Summit
Ten Greenway Plaza
Houston, TX 77046
(713) 627-0600

Exec. VP/Business Operations .... John Thomas
CFO .... Michael Barth
VP/Broadcasting and Sales .... Tom Cordova
VP/Customer Services .... Brenda Tinnen
Dir./Communications .... Linda Sease
Dir./Ticket Sales .... Nick Ueber

INDIANA PACERS

300 E. Market St.
Indianapolis, IN 46204
(317) 263-2100

President .... Donnie Walsh
VP/Administration .... Dale Ratermann
VP/Basketball .... Billy Knight
CFO .... Bob Metelko
Controller .... Doug McKee
Dir./Media Relations .... David Benner
Dir./Community Relations .... Kathy Jordan
Dir./Ticket Sales .... Mike Henn
Dir./Sponsorship Sales .... Keith Hendricks
Dir./Broadcast, Cable .... Larry Mago
Dir./Merchandise .... Rich Kapp
Dir./Advertising .... Wendy Sommers
Dir./Game Operations .... Barry Donovan

LOS ANGELES CLIPPERS

L.A. Memorial Sports Arena
3939 S. Figueroa St.
Los Angeles, CA 90037
(213) 745-0400

Exec. VP .... Andy Roeser
VP/Communications .... Joe Safety
VP/Marketing & Broadcasting ..... Mitch Huberman
VP/Marketing .... Carl Lahr
Controller .... Amy Fowler
Dir./Sponsor Services .... Diane Thibert
Dir./Promotions .... Lou Rosenberg

LOS ANGELES LAKERS

Great Western Forum
3900 W. Manchester Blvd.
Inglewood, CA 90306
(310) 419-3100

President .... Lou Baumeister
CEO .... Frank Mariani
Exec. VP/Basketball Operations .... Jerry West
GM .... Mitch Kupchak
Exec. VP .... Ken Doi
VP/Finance .... Joe McCormack
Controller .... Ross Cote
Dir./Sales .... Steve Chase
Dir./Combination Sales .... John Roth
Dir./Marketing and Broadcasting .... Keith Harris
Dir./Public Relations .... John Black

MIAMI HEAT

The Miami Arena
Miami, FL 33136-4102
(305) 577-4328

Exec. VP .... Pauline Winick
VP/Finance .... Sammy Schulman
VP/Sponsor Relations .... Joy Behrman
VP/Community Relations .... Wali Jones
Dir./Public Relations .... Mark Pray
Dir./Corporate Education .... Sybil Wilson-George
Dir./Marketing and Community
  Services .... Jorge Cunill
Dir./Customer Relations .... Jeff Craney
Dir./Community Sales Dvlpmt. .... Mercy Alvarez
Dir./Sales .... Mike Weiss
Dir./Sponsor Relations .... Terry Touchton
Dir./Team Services and Info. .... Andy Elisburg

MILWAUKEE BUCKS

Bradley Center
1001 N. Fourth St.
Milwaukee, WI 53203
(414) 227-0500

President .... Herb Kohl
VP of Basketball Operations/
  Head Coach .... Mike Dunleavy
VP/Business Operations .... John Steinmiller
Dir./Finance .... Jim Woloszyk
Dir./Publicity .... Bill King II
Dir./Sales .... Jim Grayson
Dir./Team Services .... Tom Hoffer

MINNESOTA TIMBERWOLVES

Target Center
600 First Ave. North
Minneapolis, MN 55403
(612) 673-1600

President .... Bob Stein
GM .... Phil Saunders
VP/Marketing and Sales .... Chris Wright
CFO & VP/Administration .... Joe Pettirossi
Mgr./Media Services .... Kent Wipf
Mgr./Broadcasting .... Charley Frank
Mgr./Ticket Sales .... Jeff Munneke
Mgr./Audio-Visual .... Duffer Schultz
Mgr./Community Relations .... Bill McMoore

NEW JERSEY NETS

405 Murray Hill Parkway
East Rutherford, NJ 07073
(201) 935-8888

President & COO .... Jon Spoelstra
GM .... Willis Reed
Exec. VP/Operations .... Jim Lampariello
Sr. VP/Finance & Controller .... Ray Schaetzle
VP/Ticket Operations .... Jim Leahy
VP/Sponsorship Sales .... Lou Terminello
VP/Sponsorship Programs .... Brett Yormark
VP/Ticket Operations .... Kati Kaiser
Dir./Public Relations ....John Mertz
Dir./International Marketing .... Yoshi Okamoto

NEW YORK KNICKS

Madison Square Garden
Two Pennsylvania Plaza
New York, NY 10121
(212) 465-6000

President .... David Checketts
VP and GM .... Ernie Grunfeld
VP and General Counsel .... Kenneth Munoz
VP/Public Relations .... John Cirillo
VP/Business Mgr. .... Francis Murphy
Dir./Administration .... Ed Tapscott
Dir./Marketing .... Pam Harris
Dir./Publications-Inform. .... Dennis D'Agostino
Dir./Community Relations .... Cal Ramsey
Dir./Public Relations .... Chris Brienza

ORLANDO MAGIC

One Magic Place
Orlando Arena
Orlando, FL 32801
(407) 649-3200

President .... Bob Vander Weide
GM/COO ....Pat Williams
Exec. VP/Business Operations .... Jack Swope
VP/Marketing/Administration .... Cari Coats
Dir./Sponsorship-Broadcast Sales .... Edgar Allen
Dir./Box Office Operations .... Ashleigh Bizzelle
Dir./Broadcasting .... John Cook
Dir./Novelty Sales .... Kathy Farkas
Dir./Finance .... Scott Herring
Dir./Publicity-Media Relations .... Alex Martins
Controller .... Jim Fritz

PHILADELPHIA 76ERS

Veterans Stadium
P.O. Box 25040
Philadelphia, PA 19147
(215) 339-7600

VP .... David Katz
GM/Head Coach/VP-Basketball .... John Lucas
Dir./Broadcast Sales .... Fred Liedman
Dir./Community Relations .... Steve Mix
Dir./Corporate Sales .... J. Scott Loft
Dir./Group Sales .... Ron Dick
Dir./Marketing .... Alan Sharavsky
Dir./Promotions .... Toni Amendolia-Carelli
Dir./Public Relations-Publicity .... Joe Favorito
Dir./Statistical Information .... Harvey Pollack
Dir./Ticket Sales .... Karen Gallagher

PHOENIX SUNS

201 E. Jefferson
Phoenix, AZ 85004
(602) 379-7900

President & CEO .... Jerry Colangelo
Sr. Exec. VP .... Cotton Fitzsimmons
VP/COO .... Richard Dozer
VP/Asst. GM .... Bryan Colangelo
VP/Marketing .... Harvey Shank
VP/Public Relations .... Tom Ambrose
VP/Broadcasting .... Al McCoy
Controller .... Jim Pitman
Dir./Game Operations .... Kenny Glenn
Dir./Ticket Operations .... Dianne Yeager
Media Relations Dir. .... Julie Fie
Community Relations Dir. .... Rob Harris
Dir./Merchandising .... Scott Blanford
Dir./Corporate Sales .... Cathy Hughes
Publications Dir. .... Jim Brewer
Human Resources Dir. .... Cheryl Naumann
Dir./Info. Services .... William Bolt

PORTLAND TRAIL BLAZERS

700 N.E. Multnomah St., Suite 600
Portland, OR 97232
(503) 234-9291

President/Basketball .... Bob Whitsitt
President/Business Affairs .... Marshall Glickman
VP/General Counsel .... Mike Fennell
VP/Player Personnel .... Brad Greenberg
VP/Finance .... Charlene Hodges
VP/Marketing .... Larry Hitchcock
VP/Customer and Ticket Service ...... Berlyn Hodges
VP/Sales and Client Services .... Tom McDonald
VP/Special Events .... Wally Scales
VP/Business Development .... J. Isaac
Dir./Media Services .... John Christensen
Dir./Community Affairs .... Jim Taylor
Dir./Client Services .... Marta Monetti
Dir./Sales .... Erin Hubert
Dir./Creative Services .... Sharon Higdon
Dir./Game Operations .... Jose Ayala
Controller .... Linda Glasser

SACRAMENTO KINGS

One Sports Parkway
Sacramento, CA 95834
(916) 928-0000

President .... Rick Benner
VP/Corporate Sales .... Joe Marsalla
VP/Finance .... Steve Schmidt
VP/Marketing-Broadcasting .... Mike McCullough
Dir./Customer Relations .... Philip Hess
Dir./Creative Services .... Michael Hansen
Dir./Marketing .... Sally Simonds
Dir./Media Relations .... Travis Stanley
Dir./Community Relations .... Cathy Betts
Dir./Business Operations .... Marie Nicholson
Dir./Broadcast Operations .... Kurt Eichsteadt
Dir./Merchandising .... Bruce Richards
Dir./Broadcast Sales .... Sarah Simpson
Dir./Ticket Sales .... Michael Arya

SAN ANTONIO SPURS

Alamodome
100 Montana St.
San Antonio, TX 78203
(210) 544-7700

President/CEO .... John Diller
Exec. VP/Business Operations ...... Russ Bookbinder
Sr. VP/Broadcasting .... Lawrence Payne
VP/CFO .... Rick Pych
VP/Adm.-Communications .... Larry Alexander
VP/Marketing .... Bruce Guthrie
VP/Sales .... Joe Clark
Dir./Community Relations .... Alison Fox
Dir./Media Services .... Tom James
Dir./Human Resources .... Paula Winslow

SEATTLE SUPERSONICS

190 Queen Anne Ave. N., Suite 200
Seattle, WA 98109
(206) 281-5800

President and GM .... Wally Walker
Exec. VP .... John Dresel
VP/Finance .... Brian Dixon
Sr. VP/Sales .... Laura Kussick
VP/Corporate Sponsorships
  and Broadcast .... Scott Patrick
VP/Game Operations .... Rob Martin
VP/Marketing and Promotions .... Pam Malone
Dir./Marketing and Promotions .... Linda Connors
Dir./Corporate Sponsorships
  and Broadcast .... Doug Ramsey
Dir./Community Relations .... Jim Marsh
Dir./Merchandising .... Andrew Fischer
Dir./Media Relations .... Cheri White
Dir./Sales .... Bob Boustead
Dir./Ticket Operations .... Kathy Coddington

TORONTO RAPTORS

20 Bay St., #1702
Toronto, Ontario
Canada M5J 2N8

President .... John Bitove
VP/Business Development .... Brian Cooper
VP/Finance .... Dan Durso
Dir./Broadcasting .... Chris McCracken
Dir./Corporate Partnerships .... Steve Webber
Dir./Consumer Products .... David Strickland
Dir./Ticketing .... Mark Lavaway
Dir./Communications .... John Lashway

UTAH JAZZ

Delta Center
301 West So. Temple
Salt Lake City, UT 84101
(801) 325-2500

GM .... R. Tim Howells
President .... Frank Layden
VP/Public Relations-Spec. Events .... David Allred
VP/Sales .... Larry Baum
VP/Marketing .... Jay Francis
VP/Finance-Retail Operations .... Bob Hyde
VP/Broadcasting-Nat. Sales Mgr. .... Randy Rigby
Dir./Broadcasting .... Brian Douglas
Dir./Store Operations .... Hayden Felt
Dir./Promotions .... Grant Harrison
Dir./Information .... Mark Kelly
Dir./Group Ticket Sales .... Mike Kuetell
Dir./Retail Purchasing .... Marty Olson
Dir./Local Sales .... Mike Snarr
Dir./Media Services .... Kim Turner
Dir./Customer Service Center .... Nola Wayman
Dir./Youth Basketball Programs .... David Wilson

VANCOUVER GRIZZLIES

Third Floor
780 Beatty St.
Vancouver, B.C.
Canada V6B 2M1
(604) 681-2226

GM/VP Basketball Operations .... Stu Jackson
VP/Finance-Administration .... David Cobb
VP/Communications .... Tom Mayenknecht
VP/Sales .... John Rizzardini
Dir./Marketing .... John Rocha
Dir./Ticket Sales .... Dave Smrek
Dir./Special Events and Game
    Operations .... Greg von Schottenstein

WASHINGTON BULLETS

USAir Arena
Landover, MD 20785
(301) 773-2255

President .... Susan O'Malley
Exec. VP .... Wes Unseld
VP/GM .... John Nash
VP .... Judy Holland
VP .... Rick Moreland
Exec. Dir./Customer Service .... Rhonda Ballute
Controller .... Pinky Bacsinila
Dir./Corp. Marketing .... Lee Stacey
Dir./Communications .... Matt Williams

NATIONAL FOOTBALL LEAGUE

410 Park Ave.

New York, NY 10022

(212) 758-1500

ARIZONA CARDINALS

P.O. Box 888
Phoenix, AZ 85001
(602) 379-0101

President .... William Bidwell
Exec. VP .... Joe Rhein
Head Coach/GM .... Buddy Ryan
VP .... Larry Wilson
General Counsel .... Thomas Guilfoil
CFO ....Charley Schlegel
Asst. GM ....Bob Ackles
Dir./Broadcast Sales .... John Shean
Dir./Public Relations .... Paul Jensen
Dir./Community Relations .... Adele Harris
Dir./Marketing .... Joe Castor
Ticket Mgr. .... Steve Walsh

ATLANTA FALCONS

2745 Burnette Rd.
Suwanee, GA 30174
(404) 945-1111

President .... Taylor Smith
CFO ....Jim Hay
VP/Player Personnel .... Ken Herock
Dir./Public Relations .... Charlie Taylor
Dir./Administration .... Rob Jackson
Dir./Community Relations .... Carol Breeding
Dir./Ticket Operations .... Jack Ragsdale
Controller .... Wallace Norman

BUFFALO BILLS

One Bills Dr.
Orchard Park, NY 14127
(716) 648-1800

President .... Ralph C. Wilson
Exec. VP/GM .... John Butler
Dir./Business Operations ....Jim Overdorf
Dir./Marketing-Sales .... John Livsey
Dir./Merchandising .... Christy Wilson Hofmann
Dir./Player-Alumni Relations .... Jerry Butler
Dir./Public-Community Relations .... Denny Lynch
Dir./Media Relations .... Scott Berchtold
Dir./Stadium Operations .... George Koch
Dir./Security .... Bill Bambach
Ticket Dir. ....June Foran

CAROLINA PANTHERS

227 W. Trade St.
Charlotte, NC 28202
(704) 358-1644

President .... Mike McCormack
General Counsel .... Richard Thigpen, Jr.
CFO .... David Olsen
Dir./Business Operations .... Mark Richardson
Dir./Stadium Operations .... Jon Richardson
Dir./Communic.-Broadcasting .... Charlie Dayton
Dir./Sales .... Phil Youtsey
Controller .... Lisa Garber

CHICAGO BEARS

250 N. Washington Rd.
Lake Forest, IL 60045
(708) 295-6600

President-CEO .... Michael B. McCaskey
VP .... Tim McCaskey
VP/Operations .... Ted Phillips
Dir./Administration .... Tim LeFevour
Dir./Community Relations .... Pat McCaskey
Dir./Marketing-Communications .... Ken Valdiserri
Dir./Public Relations .... Bryan Harlan
Ticket Mgr. .... George McCaskey

CINCINNATI BENGALS

200 Riverfront Stadium
Cincinnati, OH 45202
(513) 621-3550

President/GM .... Michael Brown
VP .... John Sawyer
Business Mgr. .... Bill Connelly
Public Relations Dir. .... Jack Brennan
Accountant .... Jay Reis
Ticket Mgr. .... Paul Kelly

CLEVELAND BROWNS

P.O. Box 679
Berea, OH 44017
(216) 891-5000

Owner/President .... Arthur B. Modell
Exec. VP/Legal-Administration .... Jim Bailey
VP/Asst. to President .... David Modell
VP/Public Relations .... Kevin Byrne
Dir./Marketing .... Gary Gottfried
Dir./Tickets .... Bill Breit
Dir./Operations-Information .... Bob Eller
Dir./Business Operations .... Pat Moriarty
Player Relations/Media Services .... Dino Lucarelli
Treasurer .... Mike Srsen

DALLAS COWBOYS

One Cowboys Parkway
Irving, TX 75063
(214) 556-9900

Owner/President/GM .... Jerry Jones
VP .... Stephen Jones
VP .... Mike McCoy
VP/Marketing .... George Hays
Dir./Public Relations .... Rich Dalrymple
Dir./Operations .... Bruce Mays
Coordinator/Marketing and
    Special Events .... Charlotte Anderson

DENVER BRONCOS

13655 Broncos Parkway
Englewood, CO 80112
(303) 649-9000

President/CEO .... Pat Bowlen
GM .... John Beake
CFO/Treasurer .... Robert Hurley
Dir./Media Relations .... Jim Saccomano
Asst. to GM/Community Rel. .... Fred Fleming
Ticket Mgr. .... Gail Stuckey
Dir./Operations .... Bill Harpole
Dir./Marketing .... Rosemary Manratty

DETROIT LIONS

1200 Featherstone Rd.
Pontiac, MI 48342
(313) 335-4131

Owner/President .... William Clay Ford
Exec. VP/COO .... Chuck Schmidt
VP/Adm.-Communications .... Bill Keenist
Controller-Travel Coord. .... Tom Lesnau
Dir./Marketing, Sales and
    Ticket Operations .... Fred Otto
Dir./Marketing .... Steve Harms
Dir./Community Relations .... Tim Pendell
Media Relations Coord. .... Mike Murray
Mgr./Promotions .... Paula Buckhaulter

GREEN BAY PACKERS

1265 Lombardi Ave.
Green Bay, WI 54304
(414) 496-5700

President/CEO .... Robert Harlan
VP/Administration .... Michael Reinfeldt
Exec. VP/GM .... Ron Wolf
Exec. Asst. to President .... Phil Pionek
Exec. Dir./Public Relations .... Lee Remmel
Dir./Marketing .... Jeff Cieply
Dir./Community Relations .... Mark Schiefelbein
Ticket Dir. .... Mark Wagner
Controller .... Dick Blasczyk
Dir./Computer Operations .... Wayne Wichlacz

HOUSTON OILERS

6910 Fannin St., Lower Level
Houston, TX 77030
(713) 797-9111

President	Bud Adams, Jr.
Exec. VP/GM	Floyd Reese
Exec. VP/Administration	Mike McClure
Exec. VP/Finance	Scott Thompson
Exec. Asst. to President	Thomas Smith
VP/General Counsel	Steve Underwood
Sr. VP/Marketing-Broadcast	Don MacLachlan
Dir./Business Operations	Lewis Mangum
Dir./Media Services	Dave Pearson
Dir./Accounting Services	Marilan Logan
Controller	Jackie Curley
Dir./Ticket Adm. Services	Mike Mullis
Dir./Security	Grady Sessums
Dir./Computer Services	Steve Reese
Dir./Player Relations	Willie Alexander

INDIANAPOLIS COLTS

P.O. Box 535000
Indianapolis, IN 46253
(317) 297-2658

President	Robert Irsay
VP/GM	Jim Irsay
VP/Football Operations	Bill Tobin
VP/General Counsel	Michael Chernoff
Asst. GM	Bob Terpening
Controller	Kurt Humphrey
Dir./Operations	Pete Ward
Dir./Public Relations	Craig Kelley
Ticket Mgr.	Larry Hall
Dir./Sales	Rene Longoria

JACKSONVILLE JAGUARS

1 Stadium Place
Jacksonville, FL 32202
(904) 633-6000

President/COO	David Seldin
General Counsel	Paul Vance
Sr. VP/Marketing	Dan Connell
VP/Broadcasting and Creative Services	Peter Scheurmier
VP/Ticket Operations	Judy Seldin
Exec. Dir./Communications	Dan Edwards
Dir./Finance	David Blasic
Dir./Corporate Sponsorship	David Rowan
Dir./Special Events-Promotions	Ann Carroll

KANSAS CITY CHIEFS

One Arrowhead Dr.
Kansas City, MO 64129
(816) 924-9300

President/GM/COO	Carl Peterson
Exec. VP	Tim Connolly
Asst. GM	Dennis Thum
Dir./Finance-Treasurer	Dale Young
Dir./Public Relations	Bob Moore
Dir./Operations	Jeff Klein
Dir./Marketing-Sales	Dennis Watley
Dir./Development	Ken Blume
Dir./Promotions	Phil Thomas
Mgr./Community Relations	Brenda Sniezek
Ticket Mgr.	Dave Hopkins

MIAMI DOLPHINS

2269 N.W. 199th St.
Miami, FL 33056
(305) 452-7000

President	Timothy Robbie
Exec. VP	Daniel Robbie
Exec. VP	Janet Robbie
Exec. VP/GM	Eddie Jones
General Counsel	Jann Iliff
Treasurer	Jill Strafaci
Asst. GM	Bryan Wiedmeier
Dir./Facility Operations	John Glode
Dir./Media Relations	Harvey Greene
Dir./Marketing	David Evans
Dir./Community Relations	Fudge Browne
Ticket Dir.	Lamar Vernon
Sales Dir.	Lynn Abramson

MINNESOTA VIKINGS

9520 Viking Dr.
Eden Prairie, MN 55344
(612) 828-6500

President/CEO	Roger Headrick
VP Adminis.-Team Operations	Jeff Diamond
Dir./Finance	Nick Valentine
Dir./Research-Development	Mike Eayrs
Dir./Marketing	Kernal Buhler
Dir./Public Relations	David Pelletier
Dir./Team Operations	Breck Spinner
Ticket Mgr.	Harry Randolph
Dir./Security	Steve Rollins

NEW ENGLAND PATRIOTS

Foxboro Stadium, Rte. 1
Foxboro, MA 02035
(508) 543-8200

President/CEO .... Robert Kraft
VP/Business Operations .... Andrew Wasynczuk
VP/Finance .... James Hausmann
VP/Event Management .... Brian O'Donovan
Corporate Marketing and Sales .... Daniel Kraft
Dir./Public-Community Rel. .... Donald Lowery
Dir./Data Processing .... Peg Myers
Controller .... Virginia Widman
Dir./Ticketing .... Ken Sternfeld
Marketing Mgr. .... Mitch Hardin

NEW ORLEANS SAINTS

901 Papworth Ave.
Metairie, LA 70005
(504) 733-0255

Exec. VP/Administration .... Jim Miller
VP/Marketing .... Greg Suit
Comptroller .... Charleen Sharpe
Dir./Corporate Sales .... Bill Ferrante
Dir./Media Relations .... Rusty Kasmiersky
Dir./Travel, Entertainment
  and Special Projects .... Barra Birrcher
Dir./Community Relations .... Chanel Lagarde
Ticket Mgr. .... Sandy King

NEW YORK GIANTS

Giants Stadium
East Rutherford, NJ 07073
(201) 935-8111

VP/GM .... George Young
Asst. GM .... Harry Hulmes
Controller .... John Pasquali
Dir./Administration .... Tom Power
Sr. Dir./Marketing .... Rusty Hawley
Dir./Promotion .... Frank Mara
Ticket Mgr. .... John Gorman
Dir./Public Relations .... Pat Hanlon

NEW YORK JETS

1000 Fulton Ave.
Hemstead, NY 11550
(516) 538-6600

President .... Steve Gutman
VP/GM .... Dick Steinberg
Asst. GM .... James Harris
Dir./Public Relations .... Frank Ramos
Travel Coord. .... Kevin Coyle
Treasurer & CFO .... Mike Gerstle
Controller ....Mike Minarczyk
Dir./Operations .... Mike Kensil
Exec. Dir./Business Operations .... Bob Parente
Marketing Mgr. .... Bruce Popko
Ticket Mgr. .... Gerry Parravano

OAKLAND RAIDERS

332 Center St.
El Segundo, CA 90245
(310) 322-3451

President ....Al Davis
Exec. Asst. .... Al LoCasale
Finance .... Tom Blanda
Sr. Administrator .... Morris Bradshaw
Business Mgr. .... John Novak
Sr. Executive .... John Herrara
Publications .... Mike Taylor
Community Relations .... Gil Lafferty-Hernandez
Ticket Operations .... Peter Eiges

PHILADELPHIA EAGLES

3501 S. Broad St.
Philadelphia, PA 19148
(215) 463-2500

President/COO .... Harry Gamble
VP .... Suzi Braman
VP/CFO .... Mimi Box
VP/Sales and Development .... Decker Uhlhorn
Asst. to President .... George Azar
Dir./Public Relations .... Ron Howard
Dir./Alumni Relations-Travel .... Jim Gallagher
Dir./Administration .... Vicki Chatley
Ticket Mgr. .... Leo Carlin
Dir./Penthouse Operations .... Christiana Noyalas
Dir./Penthouse Sales .... Debbie Santore
Dir./Corporate Sales .... Scott O'Neil

PITTSBURGH STEELERS

300 Stadium Circle
Pittsburgh, PA 15212
(412) 323-1200

President	Daniel Rooney
VP	John McGinley
VP	Arthur Rooney
Dir./Communications	Joe Gordon
Controller	Michael Hagan
Business Mgr.	James Boston
Ticket Sales Mgr.	Geraldine Glenn

ST. LOUIS RAMS

100 N. Broadway, Suite 2100
St. Louis, MO 63102
(314) 982-7267

Owner/President	Georgia Frontiere
Exec. VP	John Shaw
Sr. VP	Jay Zygmunt
VP/Media-Community Rel.	Marshall Klein
Treasurer	Jeff Brewer
Dir./Operations	John Oswald
Dir./Public Relations	Rick Smith
Dir./Tickets	Mike Naughton

SAN DIEGO CHARGERS

9449 Friars Road
San Diego, CA 92108
(619) 280-2111

Chairman of the Board/President	Alex Spanos
GM	Bobby Beathard
VP/Finance	Jeremiah Murphy
Asst. GM	Dick Daniels
Coord./Football Operations	Marty Hurney
Dir./Public Relations	Bill Johnston
CFO	Jeanne Bonk
Business Mgr.	Pat Curran
Dir./Marketing	Rich Israel
Dir./Ticket Operations	Joe Scott

SAN FRANCISCO 49ERS

4949 Centennial Blvd.
Santa Clara, CA 95054
(408) 562-4949

President	Carmen Policy
VP/Business Operations and CFO	Keith Simon
Dir./Public-Community Relations	Rodney Knox
Dir./Marketing-Promotions	Laurie Albrecht
Ticket Mgr.	Lynn Carrozzi
Dir./Stadium Operations	Mo Fowell

SEATTLE SEAHAWKS

11220 N.E. 53rd St.
Kirkland, WA 98033
(206) 827-9777

President	David Behring
GM/Head Coach	Tom Flores
Exec. VP	Mickey Loomis
VP/Admin.-Public Relations	Gary Wright
Dir./Publicity	Dave Neubert
Dir./Community Relations	Sandy Gregory
Dir./Sales-Marketing	Reggie McKenzie
Dir./Data Processing	Sterling Monroe
Ticket Mgr.	James Nagaoka

TAMPA BAY BUCCANEERS

One Buccaneer Place
Tampa, FL 33607
(813) 870-2700

VP/Football Administration	Rich McKay
Dir./Ticket Sales and Operations	Rick Odioso
Dir./Public Relations	Chip Namias
Dir./Corporate Sales-Broadcasting	Jim Overton
Dir./Advertising-Sales	Paul Sickmon
Controller	Patrick Smith

WASHINGTON REDSKINS

P.O. Box 17247
Dulles Airport, DC 20041
(703) 729-7601

Chairman/CEO	Jack Kent Cooke
Exec. VP	John Kent Cooke
House Counsel	Stuart Haney
Controller	Gregory Dillon
GM	Charley Casserly
Dir./Communications	Rick Vaughn
Dir./Media Relations	Mike McCall
Dir./Information	John Autry
Dir./Stad. Op. and Prom.	John Kent Cooke, Jr.
Dir./Advertising	John Wagner
Ticket Mgr.	Jeff Ritter

NATIONAL HOCKEY LEAGUE

650 Fifth Ave., 33rd Floor

New York, NY 10019

(212) 789-2000

MIGHTY DUCKS OF ANAHEIM

2695 E. Katella Ave.
Anaheim, CA 92803
(714) 704-2700

President .... Tony Tavares
VP/GM .... Jack Ferreira
Asst. GM .... Pierre Gauthier
VP/Finance/Administration .... Andy Roundtree
Dir./Sales-Marketing .... Bill Holford
Dir./Public Relations .... Bill Robertson
Dir./Advertising Sales & Service .... Bob Wagner
Dir./Broadcasting .... Lisa Seltzer
Controller .... Martin Greenspun

BOSTON BRUINS

150 Causeway St.
Boston, MA 02114
(617) 227-3206

President and GM .... Harry Sinden
VP .... Tom Johnson
Asst. GM .... Mike O'Connell
Sr. Asst. to the President .... Nate Greenberg
Asst. to the President .... Joe Curnane
Dir./Administration .... Dale Hamilton
Dir./Media Relations .... Heidi Holland
Dir./Community Relations
    and Marketing Services .... Sue Byrne
Dir./Alumni Relations .... John Bucyk
Dir./Ticket Operations .... Matt Brennan

BUFFALO SABRES

140 Main St.
Buffalo, NY 14202
(716) 856-7300

President .... Seymour H. Knox, III
Asst. to President .... Seymour H. Knox, IV
Exec. VP/Sports Operations .... Gerry Meehan
Sr. VP/Admin.-Marketing .... George Bergantz
Sr. VP/Finance and CFO .... Dan DiPofi
Dir./Public Relations .... Steve Rossi
Dir./Ticket Sales .... Tom Pokel
Dir./Merchandising .... Julie Scully
Dir./Ticket Operations .... John Sinclair
Dir./Operations .... Stan Makowski
Dir./Corporate Relations .... Larry Playfair
Dir./Communications .... Paul Wieland
Controller .... John Cudmore

CALGARY FLAMES

P.O. Box 1450, Station M
Calgary, Alberta
Canada T2P 3B9
(403) 261-0475

President .... Bill Hay
VP/GM .... Doug Risebrough
VP/Business-Finance .... Clare Rhyasen
VP/Marketing-Broadcasting .... Lanny McDonald
Controller .... Michael Holditch
Dir./Advertising-Publishing .... Pat Halls
Dir./Public Relations .... Rick Skaggs
Mgr./Tickets .... Ann-Marie Malarchuk

CHICAGO BLACKHAWKS

1901 W. Madison St.
Chicago, IL 60612
(312) 455-7000

President .... William Wirtz
VP & Asst. to the President .... Thomas Ivan
Sr. VP/GM .... Robert Pulford
VP .... Jack Davison
VP/Marketing .... Peter Wirtz
Controller .... Robert Rinkus
Dir./Public Relations-Sales .... Jim DeMaria
Dir./Marketing-Merchandising .... Jim Sofranko
Dir./Community Relations .... Barbara Davidson
Dir./Publications .... Brad Freeman
Dir./Game Night Operations
   and Special Events .... Tom Finks
Ticket Mgr. .... Jim Bare

DALLAS STARS

901 Main St., #2301
Dallas, TX 75202
(214) 712-2890

President .... James Lites
VP/Marketing .... William Strong
VP/Advertising and Promotion .... Jeff Cogen
VP/Business Operations
   and General Counsel .... Len Perna
VP/Finance .... Rick McLaughlin
Dir./Operations .... Geoff Moore
Dir./Public Relations .... Larry Kelly
Dir./Publications .... Jacqueline Grisez
Dir./Ticket Sales .... Brian Byrnes
Dir./Advertising-Promotions .... Christy Martinez
Dir./Promotions .... Cookie Lehman
Dir./Merchandising .... Jason Siegel
Dir./Corporate Sales .... Dana Summers
Dir./Corporate Hospitality .... Jill Cogen
Dir./Ticket Operations .... Augie Manfredo

DETROIT RED WINGS

600 Civic Center Dr.
Detroit, MI 48226
(313) 396-7544

President .... Mike Ilitch
VP .... Atanas Ilitch
VP .... Christopher Ilitch
Sr. VP .... Jim Devellano
Controller .... Paul MacDonald
Public Relations Dir. .... Bill Jamieson
Broadcast Print/Sales Dir. .... Amy Goan
Marketing Dir. ....Ted Speers
Season Ticket Sales Dir. .... Tina Lasley

EDMONTON OILERS

Northlands Coliseum
Edmonton, Alberta
Canada T5B 4M9
(403) 474-8561

President/GM .... Glen Sather
Exec. VP/Asst. GM .... Bruce MacGregor
VP/Finance .... Werner Baum
Dir./Public Relations .... Bill Tuele
Dir./Community Relations
   and Special Events .... Trish Kerr
Dir./Marketing .... Stew MacDonald
Dir./Ticketing Operations .... Sheila MacDonald

FLORIDA PANTHERS

100 Northeast Third Ave., 10th Floor
Ft. Lauderdale, FL 33301
(305) 768-1900

President .... William Torrey
VP/Business-Marketing .... Dean Jordan
VP/Finance-Administration .... Jonathan Mariner
GM .... Bryan Murray
Dir./Finance-Administration .... Steve Dauria
Dir./Public-Media Relations .... Greg Bouris
Dir./Promotions-Spec. Projects .... Declan Bolger
Dir./Corporate Sales
   and Sponsorships .... Kimberly Terranova
Dir./Merchandise .... Ron Dennis
Dir./Ticket-Game Day Oper .... Steve Dangerfield

HARTFORD WHALERS

242 Trumbull St.
Hartford, CT 06103
(203) 728-3366

President/GM .... Jim Rutherford
Sr. VP/Marketing-Pub. Relations .... Russ Gregory
VP/Finance-Administration .... MichaelAmendola
VP/Marketing-Sales .... Rick Francis
Dir./Public-Media Relations ....John Forslund
Dir./Community Relations .... Mary Lynn Gorman
Dir./Publications, Statistics
   and Archives ....Frank Polnaszek
Dir./Ticket Sales .... Jim Baldwin

LOS ANGELES KINGS

P.O. Box 17013
Inglewood, CA 90308
(310) 419-3160

President	Bruce McNall
Exec. VP	Lester Wintz
VP/Finance	Michael Handelman
Dir./Media Relations	Rick Minch
Dir./Publications	Nick Salata
Dir./Marketing	Sergio Del Prado
Dir./Human Resources	Barbara Mendez
Exec. Dir./Merchandising	Harvey Boles
Exec. Dir./Sales	Dennis Metz

MONTREAL CANADIANS

2313 Ste. Catherine West
Montreal, Quebec
Canada H3H 1N2
(514) 932-2582

President	Ronald Corey
VP/Finance-Administration	Fred Steer
VP/Communications and Marketing Services	Bernard Brisset
Dir./Communications	Donald Beauchamp
Dir./Finance	Francois Trudel

NEW JERSEY DEVILS

P.O. Box 504
East Rutherford, NJ 07073
(201) 935-6050

President & GM	Louis Lamoriello
Exec. VP	Max McNab
Sr. VP/Finance	Chris Modrzynski
VP/Sales-Marketing	Michael McCall
VP/Operations-Human Resources	Peter McMullen
Dir./Media Relations	Mike Levine
Dir./Finance	Scott Struble
Dir./Promotional Marketing	Ken Ferriter
Sr. Dir./Ticket Operations	Terry Farmer

NEW YORK ISLANDERS

Nassau Veterans Memorial Coliseum
Uniondale, NY 11553
(516) 794-4100

COO	Ralph Palleschi
Exec. VP	Paul Greenwood
Sr. VP & CFO	Arthur McCarthy
VP/GM	Don Maloney
VP/Communications	Pat Calabria
VP/Media Sales	Arthur Adler
Dir./Community Relations	Maureen Brady
Dir./Game Events	Tim Breach
Dir./Media Relations	Ginger Killian Serby
Dir./Publications	Chris Botta
Dir./Administration	Joseph Dreyer
Dir./Corporate Sales	Bill Kain
Dir./Executive Suites	Tracy Matthews
Dir./Merchandising	Mike Walsh

NEW YORK RANGERS

Madison Square Garden
New York, NY 10001
(212) 465-6485

President and GM	Neil Smith
VP/Finance	Jim Abry
Dir./Communications	Barry Watkins
Dir./Marketing	Kevin Kennedy
Mgr./Community Relations	Rod Gilbert
Mgr./Promotions	Caroline Calabrese
Mgr./Marketing Operations	Jim Pfeifer
Mgr./Event Presentation	Jeanie Baumgartner

OTTAWA SENATORS

301 Promenade Moodie Dr., #200
Nepean, Ontario
Canada K2H 9C4

President, GM	Randy Sexton
Sr. VP & CFO	Bernie Ashe
VP/Finance	Jim Ablett
VP/Corporate Communications	John Owens
VP/Sales	Mark Bonneau
VP/Marketing	Jim Steel
VP/Ticket & Game Day Operations	Jeff Kyle
Dir./Community Relations	Lisa Brazeau
Dir./Media Relations	Laurent Benoit
Dir./Promotions	Patti Zebchuck
Dir./Operations, Guest Services	David Dakers
Dir./Publications	Carl Lavigne
Dir./Team-Business Development	Brad Marsh

PHILADELPHIA FLYERS

Pattison Place
Philadelphia, PA 19148
(215) 465-4500

President and GM .... Bob Clarke
COO ....Ron Ryan
Exec. VP .... Keith Allen
Exec. VP/Sales-Marketing .... Dick Deleguardia
VP/Finance .... Dan Clemmens
VP/Public Relations .... Mark Piazza
VP/Sales ....Jack Betson
Dir./Finance .... Jeff Niessen
Controller .... Michelle Hay
Dir./Marketing .... Eileen Smith
Dir./Community Relations .... Linda Panasci
Ticket Mgr. .... Cecilia Baker

PITTSBURGH PENGUINS

Gate No. 9
Civic Arena
Pittsburgh, PA 15219
(412) 642-1800

President .... Jack Kelley
Sr. Exec. VP .... Bill Barnes
Exec. VP & CFO ....Donn Patton
Exec. VP/Advertising-PHA Sports
  Marketing Ltd. .... Richard Chmura
VP/Public-Community Relations .... Phil Langan
Dir./Public Relations .... Cindy Himes
Dir./Media Relations .... Harry Sanders
Dir./Special Events .... Jamie Belo
Dir./Ticket Sales ....Jeff Mercer
Dir./Advertising Sales .... Taylor Baldwin
Dir./Suite Sales-Service .... Chuck Saller
Dir./Promotions-Advertising
  Sales Coordinator .... Amy Novak
Dir./Penvision .... Bill Miller
Dir./Merchandising-Memorabilia .... Mark Willand

QUEBEC NORDIQUES

2205 Ave. du Colisee
Quebec, Quebec
Canada G1L 4W7
(418) 529-8441

President .... MarcelAubut
VP/Adminis. and Finance .... Jean Laflamme
Controller .... Francois Bilodeau
Dir./Marketing .... Bernard Thiboutot
Dir./Sales .... Andre Lestourneau
Dir./Public Relations .... Jacques Labrie
Dir./Press Relations .... Jean Martineau

ST. LOUIS BLUES

1401 Clark Ave.
St. Louis, MO 63103
(314) 622-2500

President .... John Quinn
Exec. VP .... Ronald Caron
VP/Dir. of Sales .... Bruce Affleck
VP/Dir.-Broadcast Sales .... Matt Hyland
VP/Director of Finance and
  Administration .... Jerry Jasiek
VP/Director of Public Relations-
  Marketing .... Susie Mathieu
Dir./Promotions and Community
  Relations .... Stacy Solomon
Dir./Team Services .... Rick Meagher

SAN JOSE SHARKS

525 W. Santa Clara St.
San Jose, CA 95113
(408) 287-7070

President .... Arthur Savage
Exec. VP/COO .... Greg Jamison
VP/Broadcasting and
  Media Marketing .... Malcolm Bordelon
CFO .... Gregg Olson
Dir./Media Relations .... Ken Arnold
Dir./Executive Suite Services .... Ted Atlee
Dir./Ticket Sales .... Rich Muschell
Dir./Community Development .... Lori Smith
Dir./Broadcasting .... Mark Stulberger
Dir./Marketing .... Elaine Sullivan-Digre
Dir./Finance andAccounting .... Brent Billinger
Dir./Special Projects .... Herb Briggin

TAMPA BAY LIGHTNING

501 E. Kennedy Blvd., #175
Tampa, FL 33602
(813) 229-2658

President .... Yoshio Nakamura
Exec. VP .... Chris Phillips
Exec. VP .... Mel Lowell
CFO .... MarkAnderson
VP/Communications .... Gerry Helper
Dir./Sales .... Paul D'Aiuto
Dir./Promotions .... Mark Myron
Dir./Fan Services .... Steve Woznick
Dir./Merchandising .... Kevin Murphy
Dir./Ticket Operations .... Jeff Morander

TORONTO MAPLE LEAFS

60 Carlton St.
Toronto, Ontario
Canada M5B 1L1
(416) 977-1641

President-COO-GM .... Cliff Fletcher
Dir./Business Operations
   and Communications .... Bob Stellick
Dir./Marketing .... Bill Cluff
Controller.. Ian Clarke
Public Relations Coord. .... Pat Park
Retail Operations Mgr. .... Jeff Newman
Box Office Mgr. .... Donna Henderson

VANCOUVER CANUCKS

100 N. Renfrew St.
Vancouver, BC
Canada V5K 3N7
(604) 254-5141

President .... Pat Quinn
VP/Marketing-Communications .... Glen Ringdal
VP/Finance-Adminis. .... Carlos Mascarenhas
Dir./Media-Public Relations .... Steve Tambellini
Dir./Hockey Info. .... Steve Frost
Dir./Publishing .... Norm Jewison
Corporate Sales Mgr. .... Eric Thomsen
Ticket Mgr. .... Denise McDonald
Controller .... Dave Cobb

WASHINGTON CAPITALS

USAir Arena
1 Harry S. Truman Dr.
Landover, MD 20785
(301) 386-7000

President .... Richard Patrick
VP/Finance .... Edmund Stelzer
VP/Communications .... Ed Quinlan
VP/Marketing .... Lew Strudler
Dir./Community Relations .... Yvon Labre
Dir./Sales .... Jerry Murphy
Dir./Promotions-Advertising .... Charles Copeland
Dir./Season Subscriptions .... Joanne Kowalski
Mgr./Sponsorship Sales .... Don Gore
Merchandising Coord. .... Amy Hobbs
Ticket Operations .... Kerry Gregg
Controller .... Aggie Ballard

WINNIPEG JETS

1661 Portage Ave., 10th Floor
Winnipeg, Manitoba
Canada R3J 3T7
(204) 982-5387

President .... Barry Shenkarow
VP/Finance-Administration .... Don Binda
Dir./Hockey Info. .... Igor Kuperman
Special Events Dir. .... Lori Summers
Dir./Ticket Operations .... Dianne Gabbs
Dir./Info. System .... Doug Bergman
Dir./Team Services .... Murray Harding
Controller .... Joe Leibfried
Mgr./Retail Operations .... Val Brakel
Mgr./Marketing .... Sherri Wilson
Mgr./Ticket Sales .... Hartley Miller
Dir./Corporate Sales .... Dave Baker

106

MAJOR LEAGUE BASEBALL

350 Park Ave., 17th Floor

New York, NY 10022

(212) 339-7800

ATLANTA BRAVES

P.O. Box 4064
Atlanta, GA 30302
(404) 522-7630

President .... Stan Kasten
Exec. VP and GM .... John Schuerholz
Sr. VP-Asst. to President .... Henry Aaron
Sr. VP/Administration .... Bob Wolfe
VP/Dir. Marketing-Broadcasting .... Wayne Long
Sr. Dir./Promotions-Civic Affairs .... Miles McRea
Controller .... Chip Moore
Dir./Ticket Sales .... Paul Adams
Dir./Merchandising .... Robert Hope
Dir./Ticket Operations .... Ed Newman
Dir./Advertising .... Amy Richter
Dir./Community Relations .... Dexter Santos
Dir./Public Relations .... Jim Schultz

BALTIMORE ORIOLES

333 W. Camden St.
Baltimore, MD 21201
(410) 685-9800

GM .... Roland Hemond
Dir./Business Affairs .... Walter Gutowski
Dir./Finance .... Robert Ames
Dir./Marketing-Advertising .... Scott Nickle
Dir./Community Relations .... Julie Wagner
Dir./Computer Services .... James Kline
Dir./Ticket Operations .... Joseph Keough

BOSTON RED SOX

4 Yawkey Way
Boston, MA 02215
(617) 267-9440

CEO .... John Harrington
Exec. VP and GM .... Daniel Duquette
Exec. VP/Administration .... John Buckley
VP and CFO .... Robert Furbush
VP/Broadcasting-Special Proj. .... James Healey
VP/Marketing .... Lawrence Cancro
VP/Public Relations .... Richard Bresciani
Dir./Ticket Operations .... Joseph Helyar

CALIFORNIA ANGELS

P.O. Box 2000
Anaheim, CA 92803
(714) 937-7200

President and CEO .... Richard Brown
Exec. VP .... Jackie Autry
VP and GM .... W.J. Bavasi
VP and CFO .... Ronald Shirley
VP/Civic Affairs .... Tom Seeberg
VP/Operations .... Kevin Uhlich
VP/Marketing .... Joe Schrier
Asst. VP/Media Rel.-Broadcasting .... John Sevano
Asst. VP/Sales .... Lynn Biggs
Dir./Baseball Info. .... Larry Babcock
Dir./Marketing .... Craig Gerber
Dir./Sales .... Pennie Lundberg
Controller .... Jon Sullivan
Dir./Community Relations .... Marie Moreno

CHICAGO CUBS

1060 W. Addison St.
Chicago, IL 60613
(312) 404-2827

President and CEO .... Andrew MacPhail
GM .... Ed Lynch
Exec. VP/Business Operations .... Mark McGuire
VP/Marketing-Broadcasting .... John McDonough
Dir./Publications-Special Projects .... Ernie Roth
Dir./Ticket Operations .... Frank Maloney
Dir./Media Relations .... Sharon Pannozzo

CHICAGO WHITE SOX

333 W. 35th St.
Chicago, IL 60616
(312) 924-1000

Chairman	Jerry Reinsdorf
Vice Chairman	Eddie Einhorn
Exec. VP	Howard Pizer
Sr. VP/Major League Operations	Ron Schueler
Sr. VP/Marketing-Broadcasting	Rob Gallas
VP/Finance	Tim Buzard
Dir./Marketing-Broadcasting	Mike Bucek
Dir./Sponsorship Sales-Promos	Bob Grim
Dir./Public Relations	Doug Abel
Dir./Community Relations	Christine Makowski
Dir./Ticket Sales	Bob Voight
Dir./Ticket Operations	Bob Devoy
Dir./Management Info. Services	Don Brown
Dir./Human Resources	Moira Foy
Controller	Bill Waters

CINCINNATI REDS

100 Riverfront Stadium
Cincinnati, OH 45202
(513) 421-4510

President and CEO	Marge Schott
GM	Jim Bowden
Controller	Kevin Kreitzer
Dir./Ticket Dept.	John O'Brien
Dir./Season Ticket Sales	Pat McCaffrey
Dir./Group Sales	Barb McManus
Dir./Marketing	Chip Baker
Dir./Publicity	Jon Braude

CLEVELAND INDIANS

2401 Ontario St.
Cleveland, OH 44115
(216) 420-4200

Chairman of the Board & CEO	Richard Jacobs
Exec. VP & GM	John Hart
Exec. VP/Business	Dennis Lehman
VP/Marketing-Communications	Jeff Overton
VP	Martin Cleary
VP/Public Relations	Bob DiBiasio
VP/Finance	Ken Stefanov
Dir./Media Relations	John Maroon
Dir./Advertising	Valerie Arcuri
Dir./Corporate Marketing-Sales	Jon Starrett
Dir./Broadcasting	Mike Lehr
Dir./Ticket Services	Connie Minadeo
Dir./Ticket Sales	Vic Gregovits
Dir./Merchan.-Licensing	Jayne Churchmack
Dir./Community Relations	Allen Davis

COLORADO ROCKIES

1700 Broadway St., #2100
Denver, CO 80290
(303) 292-0200

President and CEO	Jerry McMorris
Exec. VP/Operations	John McHale
Sr. VP & GM	Bob Gebhard
Sr. VP & CFO	Hal Roth
VP/Sales-Marketing	Dave Glazier
VP/Finance	Michael Kent
VP/Operations	Keli McGregor
Sr. Dir./Ticket Sales	Sue Ann McClaren
Dir./Public Relations	Mike Swanson
Dir./Ticket Operations	Chuck Javernick
Dir./Publications	Jimmy Oldham
Dir./Community Affairs	Roger Kinney
Dir./Management Info. Systems	Mary Burns

DETROIT TIGERS

2121 Trumbull
Detroit, MI 48216
(313) 962-4000

President & CEO	John McHale, Jr.
VP	Atanas Ilitch
VP	Christopher Ilitch
Sr. Dir./GM	Joe Klein
CFO	Gerald Pasternak
Sr. Dir./Public Relations	Daniel Ewald
Dir./Marketing	Michael Dietz
Controller	Scott Fisher
Dir./Community Relations	Jim Price
Dir./Ticket Operations	Ken Marchetti
Dir./Ticket Sales	Gino D'Ambrosio

FLORIDA MARLINS

2267 NW 199th St.
Miami, FL 33056
(305) 626-7400

President	Donald Smiley
Exec. VP and GM	David Dombrowski
VP/Business Operations	Richard Andersen
VP/Broadcasting	Dean Jordan
VP/Finance-Administration	Jonathan Mariner
VP/Sales-Marketing	Bob Kramm
Dir./Merchandising	Steve Stock
Dir./Ticket Operations	Bill Galante
Dir./International Relations	Tony Perez
Dir./Season & Group Sales	Frank Gernert
Dir./Corporate Sales-Sponsorships	Neal Bendesky
Dir./Community Relations	Jorge Arrizurieta
Dir./Media Relations	Chuck Pool

HOUSTON ASTROS

P.O. Box 288
Houston, TX 77001
(713) 799-9500

President .... Tal Smith
Sr. VP/Business Operations .... Bob McClaren
GM .... Bob Watson
Dir./Media Relations .... Rob Matwick
Dir./Marketing .... Pam Gardner
Dir./Broadcasting-Promotions .... Jamie Hildreth
Dir./Community Development .... Gene Pemberton
Dir./Advertising .... Amy Kress
Dir./Ticket Sales-Services .... Rich Fromstein
Controller .... Robert McBurnett

KANSAS CITY ROYALS

P.O. Box 419969
Kansas City, MO 64141
(816) 921-2200

President .... Mike Herman
Exec. VP and GM .... Spencer Robinson
VP .... Charles Hughes
VP/Finance .... Dale Rohr
VP/Government-Consumer Affairs .... Merle Wood
VP/Public Relations .... Dean Vogelaar
VP/Administration .... Dennis Cryder
Dir./Marketing .... Mike Behymer
Dir./Season Ticket Sales .... Joe Grigoli
Dir./Inform. Ser.-Operations .... Loretta Kratzberg
Dir./Accounting .... Patrick Fleischmann
Dir./Info. Services .... Joe Pettelkow
Dir./Ticket Operations .... Mike Naughton

LOS ANGELES DODGERS

1000 Elysian Park Ave.
Los Angeles, CA 90012
(213) 224-1500

President .... Peter O'Malley
Exec. VP .... Fred Claire
VP/Communications .... Tom Hawkins
VP/Finance .... Bob Graziano
VP/Marketing .... Barry Stockhamer
VP/Ticketing .... Walter Nash
VP/Treasurer .... Roland Seidler
Dir./Accounting-Finance .... Bill Foltz
Dir./Advertising-Special Events .... Paul Kalil
Dir./Broadcasting-Publications .... Brent Shyer
Dir./Community Relations .... Don Newcombe
Dir./Human Resources-Adminis. .... Irene Tanji
Dir./Management Info. Systems .... Mike Mularky
Dir./Publicity .... Jay Lucas
Dir./Ticket Operations .... Debra Duncan

MILWAUKEE BREWERS

P.O. Box 3099
Milwaukee, WI 53201
(414) 933-4114

President & CEO .... Bud Selig
VP/Broadcast Operations .... Bill Haig
VP/Broadcast Sales .... Mitch Nye
VP/Finance .... Dick Hoffmann
VP/Corporate Affairs .... Laurel Prieb
VP/Ticket Sales .... Jeff Eisenberg
Dir./Community Relations .... Michael Downs
Dir./Media Relations .... Jon Greenberg
Dir./Adminis.-Human Resources .... Tom Gausden
Dir./Publications .... Mario Ziino
Dir./Ticket Operations .... John Barnes

MINNESOTA TWINS

501 Chicago Ave. South
Minneapolis, MN 55415
(612) 375-1366

President .... Jerry Bell
VP/GM .... Terry Ryan
VP/Marketing-Sales .... Bill Mahre
CFO .... Kevin Mather
VP/Operations .... Matt Hoy
Dir./Media Relations .... Rob Antony

MONTREAL EXPOS

P.O. Box 500, Station M
Montreal, Quebec
Canada H1V 3P2

President .... Claude Brochu
VP and GM .... Kevin Malone
VP/Finance .... Laurier Carpentier
VP/Marketing and Comm. .... Richard Morency
VP/Business Operations .... Claude Delorme
Dir./Events .... Claudine Cook
Dir./Promotions .... Luigi Carolo
Dir./Ticket Office .... Chantal Dalpe
Dir./Media Services .... Monique Giroux
Dir./Media Relations .... Peter Loyello
Dir./Advertising .... Johanne Heroux
Dir./Merchandising .... Susan LaBlanc
Dir./Group Sales .... Ronald Martineau
Dir./Season Ticket Sales .... Claude Chabot
Dir./Fin. Planning and Admin. .... Michel Buissiere

NEW YORK METS

126th and Roosevelt Ave.
Flushing, NY 11368
(718) 507-6387

President and CEO	Fred Wilpon
Sr. VP and Treasurer	Harold O'Shaughnessy
Sr. VP and Consultant	J. Frank Cashen
VP/Broadcasting	Mike Ryan
VP/Marketing	Mark Bingham
VP/Ticket Sales-Services	Bill Ianniciello
Dir./Adminis.-Data Processing	Russ Richardson
Dir./Community Outreach	Jill Knee
Dir./Promotions	James Plummer
Dir./Media Relations	Jay Horwitz
Dir./Ticket Operations	Dan DeMato

NEW YORK YANKEES

Yankee Stadium
Bronx, NY 10451
(718) 293-4300

Owner	George Steinbrenner
VP and GM	Gene Michael
VP/Finance-CFO	Barry Pincus
VP	Ed Weaver
VP/Ticket Operations	Frank Swaine
Dir./Office Admin. and Services	Harvey Winston
Dir./Customer Services	Joel White
Exec. Dir./Ticket Operations	Jeff Kline
Dir./Media Relations-Publicity	Rob Butcher
Dir./Marketing	Debbie Tymon
Dir./Special Events	Bob Pelegrino
Dir./Public-Community Relations	Brian Smith
Dir./Publications	Tom Bannon

OAKLAND A's

Oakland Coliseum
Oakland, CA 94621
(510) 638-4900

President and GM	Sandy Alderson
VP/Business Operations	Alan Ledford
VP/Finance	Kathleen McCracken
VP/Adminis.-Personnel	Raymond Krise Jr.
Dir./Baseball Info.	Jay Alves
Dir./Community Relations	Christina Centeno
Dir./Public Affairs	Dave Perron
Dir./Broadcast Operations	Bill King
Dir./Broadcasting	Ken Pries
Dir./Ticket Sales	John Kamperschroer
Dir./Corporate Sales	Doug Nelson
Dir./Purchasing-Merchandising	David Alioto
Dir./Group Sales-Season Tickets	Bettina Flores
Dir./Ticket Operations	Shelley Landeros

PHILADELPHIA PHILLIES

P.O. Box 7575
Philadelphia, PA 19101
(215) 463-6000

President/CEO	Bill Giles
Exec. VP and COO	David Montgomery
Sr. VP/GM	Lee Thomas
Sr. VP/Finance-Planning	Jerry Clothier
VP/Public Relations	Larry Shenk
VP/Marketing	Dennis Mannion
VP/Ticket Sales-Operations	Richard Deats
Dir./Sales	Rory McNeil
Dir./Ticket Dept.	Dan Goroff
Dir./Community Relations	Regina Castellani
Dir./Info. Systems	Brian Lamoreaux

PITTSBURGH PIRATES

P.O. Box 7000
Pittsburgh, PA 15212
(412) 323-5000

President and CEO	Mark Sauer
Sr. VP and GM	Cam Bonifay
VP/Finance-Administration	Kenneth Curcio
VP/Broadcasting-Advertising Sales	Mark Driscoll
VP/Marketing-Operations	Steven Greenberg
Sr. Dir./Sales-Marketing	Bob Derda
Dir./Ticket Operations	Gary Remlinger
Dir./Community Rel./Spec. Events	Kathy Guy
Dir./Corporate Relations	Nellie Briles
Dir./Finance	Jim Plake
Dir./Info. Systems	Sanjay Chakrabarty
Dir./In-Game Entertainment	Mike Gordon
Dir./Media Relations	Jim Trdinich
Dir./Merchandising	Joe Billetdeaux

ST. LOUIS CARDINALS

250 Stadium Plaza
St. Louis, MO 63102
(314) 421-3060

President	Mark Lamping
VP/Business Operations	Mark Gorris
Controller	Brad Wood
VP/GM	Walt Jocketty
VP/Marketing	Marty Hendin
Dir./Broadcasting and Market Development	Dan Farrell
Dir./Group Sales	Joe Strohm
Dir./Target Marketing	Ted Savage
Dir./Ticket Systems	Josephine Arnold
Dir./Human Resources	Marian Rhodes
Dir./Ticket Services	Kevin Wade

SAN DIEGO PADRES

P.O. Box 2000
San Diego, CA 92112
(619) 283-4494

President .... Dick Freeman
Exec. VP .... Bill Adams
VP/Marketing .... Don Johnson
VP/Game Operations-Special Events .... Andy Strasberg
VP/Finance .... Bob Wells
VP/Public Affairs .... Charles Steinberg
Dir./Administrative Services .... Lucy Freeman
Dir./Media Relations-Team Travel .... Roger Riley
Dir./Ticket Operations .... Dave Gilmore
Dir./Ticket Sales .... Jack Autry
Dir./Video-Special Projects .... Mark Guglielmo
Dir./Merchandising .... Michael Babida
Dir./Corporate Sales .... Michael Dee

SAN FRANCISCO GIANTS

Candlestick Park
San Francisco, CA 94124
(415) 468-3700

President .... Peter Magowan
Exec. VP .... Larry Baer
Sr. VP and GM .... Bob Quinn
Sr. VP/Business Operations .... Pat Gallagher
VP/Finance .... John Yee
Dir./Public Relations and Community
  Development .... Bob Rose
Dir./Marketing .... Mario Alioto
GM/Retail .... Connie Kullberg
Dir./Legal-Governmental Affairs .... Jack Bair

SEATTLE MARINERS

P.O. Box 4100
Seattle, WA 98104
(206) 628-3555

President and COO .... Chuck Armstrong
VP/Communications .... Randy Adamack
VP/Finance-Administration .... Brian Beggs
VP/Business Development .... Paul Isaki
VP/Marketing and Sales .... Bob Gobrecht
Controller .... Denise Podosek
Dir./Community Relations .... Joe Chard
Dir./Team Travel .... Craig Detwiler
Dir./Sales .... Beth Wojick
Dir./Marketing .... David Venneri
Dir./Public Relations .... Dave Aust
Dir./Strategic Planning .... Tim Kornegay

TEXAS RANGERS

P.O. Box 90111
Arlington, TX 76004
(817) 273-5222

President .... J. Thomas Schieffer
VP/GM .... Douglas Melvin
VP/Business Operations .... John McMichael
VP/Marketing .... David Dziedzic
VP/Administration .... Charles Wagner
VP/Public Relations .... John Blake
VP/Ballpark Development .... Jack Hill
VP/Community Development .... Norman Lyons
VP/Legal Affairs .... William Miller
Controller .... Steve McNeill
Dir./Corporate Marketing .... Dave Fendrick
Dir./In-Park Entertainment .... Chuck Morgan
Dir./Merchandising .... Nancy McCusker
Dir./Customer Relations .... Jay Miller
Dir./Ticket Operations .... John Schriever
Dir./Sales .... Ross Scott
Dir./Player Relations .... Taunee Paur
Dir./Publications .... Eric Kolb
Dir./Spanish Broadcasting and Latin
  American Liaison .... Luis Mayoral

TORONTO BLUE JAYS

1 Blue Jay Way, #3200
Toronto, Ontario
Canada M5V 1J1
(416) 341-1000

President and CEO .... Paul Beeston
VP/GM .... Gord Ash
Dir./Public Relations .... Howard Starkman
Dir./Stadium-Ticket Operations .... George Holm
Dir./Marketing .... Paul Markle
Dir./Finance .... Susie Quigley

Split the Uprights with Masters Press!

Masters Press has a complete line of books that cover football and other sports to help coaches and participants alike "master their game." All of our books are available at better bookstores or by calling Masters Press at 1-800-9-SPORTS. Catalogs available by request.

Coaching Football
*Tom Flores &
Bob O'Connor*
Trace the development of the game from the past to the present to the future and include the latest innovative plays.
$14.95, ISBN 0-940279-71-1

Conditioning for Football
Tom Zupancic
Helps coaches and players develop a program that improves performance and safety with unique methods of motivation.
$12.95, ISBN 0-940279-77-0

Youth League Football
*Tom Flores &
Bob O'Connor*
Presents drills and coaching suggestions for every position on the field, while emphasizing that you football's main objective is fun! Part of the Spalding Youth League Series.
$12.95, ISBN0-940279-69-X

Football Drill Book
Doug Mallory
Includes offensive and defensive skill drills and overall conditioning tips.
$12.95, ISBN0-940279-72-X

All-Pro Recipes: Great "Chefs" of the NFL
Features favorite recipes from more than 100 current and former NFL stars. It's a cookbook with delicious recipes, and basic cooking tips; and a sports book with a brief biography and photo of the recipe's originator. Also includes a glossary of cooking terms and equivalency chart.
$14.95, ISBN 1-57028-058-4

Call Toll Free 1-800-9-SPORTS To Order

Success is a Slam Dunk with Masters Press